I0070773

WORM ON A CHOPSTICK

*Understanding Today's Fast Moving Entrepreneurial Age:
New Directions, Strategies, Management Perspectives*

PAUL B. SILVERMAN

*Experience is not what happens to a man. It is what a
man does with what happens to him*

Aldous Huxley

ISBN: 0983537402
ISBN-13: 978-0-9835374-0-3
Library of Congress Control Number: 2011927091

Copyright Notice   Copyright © 2011   Paul B. Silverman
All rights reserved. No part of this publication may be reproduced or distributed in any form or by any means, or stored in a database or retrieval system, without the prior written consent of Gemini Business Press.

Published By

Gemini Business Press

Gemini Business Press is an imprint of Gemini Business Group, LLC
Gemini Business Press
Box 2921
Reston, VA 20195

*A portion of the proceeds from all book sales
is being donated to the American Cancer Society.*

What Readers Are Saying About
Worm on a Chopstick

"Sometimes a dynamic book comes along that makes you think in new directions, create new ideas, develop new perspectives. *Worm on a Chopstick* by Paul Silverman accomplishes this and so much more. He brings a highly experienced voice to today's entrepreneurial age discussions and lets us know where we are heading. A powerful book that could change your life."

Rita Cosby   Award Winning TV Host and Bestselling Author of *"Quiet Hero: Secrets from My Father's Past"*

"*Worm on a Chopstick* provides a solid juxtaposition of theory and practice--tempered by experience. Very readable; and a learning opportunity."

Michael W. Wynne   Investor, 21st Secretary of the Air Force, Former Undersecretary Acq Tech and Logistics

----

"A slam dunk of a book for aspiring entrepreneurs. Paul Silverman has completed 'the cycle'- businessman and teacher- and brings his relevant experience to entrepreneurs who are seeking practical advice on how to be a successful risk taker."

Tom McMillen   Former Congressman, Olympian, NBA star, and businessman

----

"*Worm on a Chopstick* elegantly combines a highly readable mixture of business "war stories" with relevant management theory. A very useful guidebook for entrepreneurs and recent business school graduates."

Jay Wright   Co-author of "*Finance and Accounting for Nonfinancial Managers, 6th edition*"

"A great read for every technology guru contemplating the next big idea...*Worm on a Chopstick* provides the business principles every young entrepreneur needs, but sometimes overlooks."

Liz Sara   High tech marketing consultant, entrepreneur, angel investor

---

"*Worm on a Chopstick*....could easily be retitled *Man on A Mission* because that is what Paul Silverman has been for 30+ years....he shares his thoughts and insights on the entrepreneurial process from every vantage point...a must read for leaders of rapid growth technology companies."

Andrew J. Sherman,   Partner, Jones Day and author of *Harvesting Intangible Assets*

"There are many management books on the market but few are presented in such a readable and understandable manner as this one. Truly a most enjoyable and worthwhile read!"

Chuck Nash   Founder and CEO Emerging Technology Inc. (ETII); retired U.S. Navy Captain and Fox News military analyst.

"Worm on a Chopstick's author, Paul Silverman, insists that in our new entrepreneurial world we must be prepared to think "out of the room" – and act strategically in the process. He uses colorful examples from his own experience as a businessman and teacher – including how to deal with a worm on his chopstick in a sticky situation – to explain how we have evolved to our current business state, the new risks and opportunities inherent in that state and approaches to addressing those risks and taking advantage of those opportunities. If you are looking to understand, survive and thrive in our new fast-paced, entrepreneurial business climate, I highly recommend *Worm on a Chopstick*."

Carl Eckstein, NextGen Capital, Managing Director

"Worm on a Chopstick provides a lifetime of business experience from the perspective of a consultant, entrepreneur and educator. It is a must-have reference for anyone in business, whether starting, running or growing a business, and those contemplating a business career. It presents in an easily readable way valuable lessons from many cases of successes and failures and will leave those who read it a basis for emulating the success stories and avoiding the costly errors of the failures. It is a recognition of the immutable foundation principles of business that must adapt to the dynamic political, economic and social forces of change in which we live now and that will apply with equal force to the succeeding generations of businessmen and women."

Ernest M. Stern, Shareholder in the corporate and securities practice group at Akerman Senterfitt LLP, a full service law firm with offices throughout the United States and the largest law firm in the State of Florida.

Excerpts from Ray Walters, *Paperback Talk* (Chicago: Academy Chicago Publishers, 1985) reviewing the paperback book revolution reproduced by permission of Academy Chicago Publishers, 363 West Erie Street, 4W, Chicago, Illinois 60654.

Excerpts from Jeffrey A. Timmons and Stephen Spinelli, *New Venture Creation: Entrepreneurship for the 21st Century*, Seventh Edition (New York: McGraw Hill/Irwin, 2007) reproduced by permission of the McGraw Hill Companies.

Excerpts from Donald A. Ball, Wendell H. McCulloch, Jr., J., Michael Geringer, Jeanne M. McNett, *International Business: The Challenge of Global Competition* (New York: McGraw Hill/Irwin, 2008), reproduced by permission of the McGraw Hill Companies.

Excerpts from *The Pleasure of Finding Things Out*, Copyright © 2005 Richard P. Feynman. Reprinted by permission of Basic Books, a member of the Perseus Books Group.

Excerpts from HILL, STRATEGIC MANAGEMENT THEORY, 5E, ©2001 South Western, a part of Cengage Learning Inc. Reproduced by permission. www.cengage.com/permissions

Excerpts from the book THE LONG TAIL by Chris Anderson. Copyright 2006 Chris Anderson. Used by permission from Hyperion. All rights reserved.

This book is dedicated to my family, who remind me what is most important in life.

First, to Dolores, for more than four decades a loving wife, soul mate, life partner, and friend. And dedicated as well to our expanding family; our children, Michele, Rob, and Steve; their spouses, Coleen and Michele; and the most important group, our grandchildren, Abby, Grace, Jackson, and Ryan. Without their collective encouragement and support, this book would not be possible.

And this book has a special dedication to my son Rob, who was taken from us all much too early and is missed dearly by his family and friends. All those he encountered in his forty-three years were positively impacted, and he will always remain in our hearts and lives.

Paul B. Silverman

Contents

Preface

No, this is not a book about the adventures of a frisky *vermes*—Latin for "worm." Nor is it a book about chopsticks or Japanese eating habits. No, *Worm on a Chopstick,* or *Chopstick* for short, is written to help readers understand and deal with today's explosive global entrepreneurial market changes, challenges, strategies, and opportunities.

And these changes are pervasive, often unexpected, and happen quickly, just like a little critter that appears on a chopstick. And these events disrupt the status quo, be it your business, your career plans, your personal life, or in my case, a planned dinner with senior executives in a downtown Tokyo restaurant.

No matter where you are in the food chain, entrepreneurial age changes impact you. Faster computers, advanced mobile devices, multimedia services, powerful new business processing tools—all factors reshaping our lives. These are what I call the "hard" changes—you can see, feel, and touch most of these. Books, articles, "talking heads" explore these changes in many channels.

"Soft" changes are another story, posing greater problems. How does technology change your world; what are the new rules to understand, survive and excel in today's explosive entrepreneurial age; where are we heading; where are the potholes we will encounter; and, most important, what new perspectives do you need to know in your job, maybe even how you think? This is *Chopstick's* target.

Chopstick's foundation builds upon my teaching, publications, presentations, and four decades of experience serving as a senior corporate executive, global management consultant, educator, public and private company CEO, entrepreneur, and mentor to many senior executives. You will also quickly see *Chopstick* uses a snappy, highly readable, no-nonsense, entertaining, anecdotal, quotable, quick-reading style—this is intentional. *Chopstick* also uses humor, entertainment, and storytelling to deliver *Chopstick*'s strong and oftentimes serious messages, techniques I have used successfully often in many global business and educational forums.

Keep in mind *Chopstick* is not a management textbook, nor does it provide technical reviews of the Internet, wireless protocols, or other jargon. If you want to understand technology, how it is changing, maybe how wireless applications will reshape health care and asset tracking systems, I can help with these but not here. I recommend you put this book back on the shelf and look elsewhere—there are many fine books that can help you, but *Chopstick* is not it. And no need to light aromatherapy candles when reading *Chopstick*. I emphasize more practical, down to earth advice and counsel based on my business and teaching experience.

Building on real experience, solving real client, global business, and people needs in a time of great change provides the foundation for what you will find in *Chopstick*. Insights and counsel are offered for surviving today's entrepreneurial age. No controlled scientific testing, no rigid formulas for success or "get rich quick" schemes here. Again, if that is what you want, wrong book—put it back on the shelf.

But if you want to glean insights, guidance, perspectives, and "war stories" from the front lines of the global entrepreneurial age to help you survive and grow, then you have come to the right place. With more than thirty-five years in the global information industry, I have managed major business for leading global companies, spent more than a decade in the global strategy management consulting arena working for clients worldwide, served as CEO and chairman of both public and private companies, published papers, and conducted presentations for diverse audiences throughout the world. And for the past eight years, I have contributed in the education sector teaching strategy management and entrepreneurship at several leading universities.

Teaching hundreds of students what I feel they need to know to understand management strategy, best practices, how to create new business while keeping "old" businesses going, working through many Harvard Business School and other case studies, also shapes many of the insights shared within *Chopstick*. I have had more than my share of wins, worked with many talented people, accomplished much. And being "at bat" perhaps more than most, I have also had my share of losses (or learning experiences as both Thomas Edison and I like to call them). Battle scars provide powerful insights, knowledge, and lessons learned. Doctors learn by working on sick people, looking at who dies and who lives. You find business often works the same way as you develop strategies and rules to address today's challenges.

I have been encouraged by many to share my perspectives and counsel, and that is one reason *Chopstick* is born. My intent here is entertainment, insights, and education, in roughly that order. Learning should be fun in my book, literally, and that is my approach in *Chopstick*.

And for those wondering, *Chopstick's* title comes from a real incident during a dinner years ago in a dimly lit Tokyo restaurant and discussed in chapter 6. Names and places changed of course. I have used this anecdote in many classroom forums to share a perspective on global business challenges, dealing with global players, cultural differences, and so on. I am not sure how many students I have either turned on or off from pursuing global business careers, but based on feedback, most have appreciated the insights. Some valuable lessons here that we will review.

So I suggest find a comfortable chair, sit back, and relax. Let me take you on a journey, and together we will explore the entrepreneurial age, look deeper on what's happening here, discuss some new ideas, and share some perspectives for survival. And most importantly, definitely have some fun along the way. I hope you enjoy the trip.

Paul B. Silverman

Introduction

You may have seen a Reuters news report in late 2010 about pills that include an embedded microchip. You swallow the "digital pill," and it captures data as it transverses your body, sends back readings to a small device you wear on your arm, links wirelessly to an iPhone or other mobile device, which sends this data to medical staff. Tiny wireless devices, pressed into traditional pills. The pills reach your stomach, batteries energized by gastric juices, data streams sent back to the device on your arm. The data can be valuable, maybe confirm you actually took your pills, what time you took the pills, what your body's reaction was, both today and tomorrow, and much more.

Think about the benefits here for clinical drug trials and those seeking to understand how and whether new drugs work. Think about how this changes patient care and the drug business. We have the ability here to create an active, real-time updated patient personal health record with "… *this is your stomach talking*" sending back data. We create the ability to alert a remote practitioner on whether a patient is experiencing a life-threatening event, such as cardiac arrest, and take immediate action, possibly dispatching emergency personnel. And think about the benefits to those having older senior relatives living alone, wondering whether they have really been taking their daily pills. The idea of "…Take two pills and have the *pills* call me in the morning" is what we are talking about here.

Digesting wireless radio devices, albeit small ones, does sound strange and may take some getting used to. Remember we are cautioned that wireless devices held close to your head may cause cancer—now we are asked to *eat* them.

I am sure this probably sounds like science fiction to many. Not really. As reported by Reuters, *Wall Street Journal,* and others, companies are developing similar technologies, and clinical trials are coming. Nanotechnology is one key technology driver here— a very exciting area reshaping many sectors. And using wireless devices to monitor patient condition promises to offer significant savings and improve our health care system, which all agree needs help.

One 2008 study estimates remote monitoring of congestive heart failure patients alone would create savings of $10.1 billion.[1] Some debate the amount of savings, but few dispute that we are creating exciting new directions to improve U.S. health care, which desperately needs it.

Take a step back from the above, take a longer view, and you realize the potential direct and ripple effect of the above technologies. Health care processes will change; how care is managed today will have to adapt. New businesses will emerge to remotely monitor and manage patients' health care; maybe offer patients virtual electronic "pill boxes" that track and report how and when pills were taken. It may sound strange now, but when a pill "calls," think about who will answer the phone, so to speak. We are changing the game here and can see new possibilities and challenges. I spend a good deal of my time looking at these and other exciting changes in all sectors.

For example, we may provide our growing senior population with new tools enabling them to stay in their homes longer. And mobile devices, iPhones and others, may serve as remote monitoring devices for tracking real time a family member's condition and whether he or she has taken their pills. Traditional communications companies may be in the health care monitoring business. I have even had some discussions related to integrating some of these new capabilities within clothing. We are not pushing the envelope here—technology exists to do this today. I would not be surprised to see a Health Monitoring Jacket sold by maybe Nordstrom and others. Sounds far out, but buying a health monitoring system off a clothing rack next to the pants nook, maybe selecting a size and color, is another example showing how today's entrepreneurial age drivers will reshape traditional sectors.

All this is coming, and much of the technology here is developed—standards, privacy, and some interworking issues must be resolved, but this is moving along quickly with many players, both small and large, involved. Solutions will be developed here.

The messages here? Change is happening and quickly; you need to develop new perspectives, consider the impact of new directions, how they will impact today's processes, what potential new directions are now enabled, what business is at risk, and so on. Let's look at this further.

Suppose you work in a major pharmaceutical firm. Do you think these developments are an opportunity or a threat? Or maybe both? How should your firm participate in this market to minimize disruption of your current business, while looking at these new opportunities? On the other hand, suppose you work in an early stage health care technology company. How can you capitalize on this disruptive innovation (more about this topic later in *Chopstick*)? What alliances and business relationships can you develop to leverage your company's technology, given these exciting new developments?

I shared with you one new technology—there are hundreds of others that are reshaping every market, every facet of business and personal lives—very exciting and promising but also challenging, forcing all, whether a major player or emerging firm, to refocus the traditional "business as usual" approach.

I discuss what I call "entrepreneurial thinking" in chapter 1, which embodies the above, proposing a new approach to help you understand and deal with today's explosive global entrepreneurial developments. That is one foundation of *Chopstick* and the intellectual thread that runs through the book.

While the health care sector is one of several areas I am involved with, *Chopstick* is not focused solely on the health care market—the above shows a dramatic health care market example of technology change driving new solutions, processes, and business models. I can easily replace the above with examples in the financial services, energy, security, retailing, and many other sectors, and we will make similar observations. No sector really escapes the global entrepreneurial market dynamics we are seeing today.

I find a good starting point is to first look at how management reacts to uncertainty and change. Not universal truths here, but perspectives I have developed based on my experience.

Today's explosive entrepreneurial age is morphing markets, companies, technologies, and industry sectors. Emerging companies are creating new market sectors. Traditional companies are often holding on to survive. Many of today's business managers are challenged, often struggling to understand what is happening and where this is all heading. I hear these messages often.

Looking deeper, I encounter two distinct management styles and perspectives driving today's businesses.

Traditional *management:* often structured, predictable, risk averse, stable, a "we will always be here" attitude. Driven by the need to address today's needs, follow traditional "it always worked before" thinking, reasonable and what most would say is today's norm for most "nine-to-five" business professionals.

Entrepreneurial *management:* often unstructured, pursuing uncharted waters, chaotic, unpredictable, uncertain, a "hope we will be here next year" attitude. Driven by unwillingness to accept the status quo, the need to change how things are done, adapt the world to *their* vision, be unreasonable, and what most would say is the norm for business professionals in "just another start-up venture." And forget the "nine-to-five" concept.

Historically, these are really two distinct worlds, two distinct sets of management thinking with well-understood rules and perspectives. No more—that was yesterday.[2]

Today's entrepreneurial age forces are smashing these two distinct management perspectives together with explosive results, reshaping all markets and every facet of our lives. *Traditional* management must develop new *entrepreneurial* management thinking or die. Look at every sector—newspapers, travel agencies, book publishing, PC software, music—these and many other traditional businesses are under entrepreneurial age "attacks."

And entrepreneurial management must quickly learn to adapt as well. The laws of *traditional* business are never repealed; violate these laws—be they marketing, financial, global strategy, or others—and you die. Strong words but look at the business failures and entrepreneurial flameouts. Building a large scale enterprise from scratch and surviving is tough work, demanding an understanding of how to manage people, address market, competition, financials, and so on—in other words, the *traditional* rules of business. The fact that more than three out of five new companies fail after three years reinforces this point. It is just as difficult to *grow* a business as it is to *launch* a new business.

Accept the above and we see the wisdom in George Bernard Shaw's observation that "reasonable men adapt to the world; unreasonable men seek to adapt the world to their vision, therefore all progress is driven by the unreasonable man" (and woman of course).

Look at the dynamics and scale here. Consider Dell, Microsoft, Home Depot, Apple, Amazon.com, and Starbucks. All created new market sectors or dramatically reshaped existing ones, and all launched as entrepreneurial ventures in only the past *thirty-five years*, some even started in a garage. Consider the Google revolution—founded in 1998 by two Stanford University students, started as a basic search engine, and within only one decade ramped up sales to $22 billion in 2008, and achieved a market cap of about $96 billion in January 2009. These dramatic examples show markets and sectors reshaping, some companies emerging, others disappearing, creating large-scale opportunities, challenging traditional business thinking.[3]

Many believe the technology sector's explosive development and growth drives our entrepreneurial age growth. True, it is sobering to think that growth of the computers, wireless services, and handheld mobile devices markets really only occurred during the past generation. I often reinforce this noting that in 1980, Microsoft looked like any of today's start-ups with about $8 million in sales and thirty-eight employees working to build their fortune.

But driven by technology and market changes, other high-potential new business sectors also emerged to drive our economic growth, and these go well beyond the high-technology sector. Think about Home Depot, which subsumed the lumberyard and hardware store sectors, and Starbucks, which created a new "recreational" coffee market. And there are other new sectors that changed how people live their lives and conduct business. Most people I find are surprised to learn that fast oil changes, convenience food superstores, pet care services, healthy living products among many others are also sectors that emerged only in the past generation.[4]

How today's two distinct management visions are morphing and merging, and the new rules, perspectives, and insights needed to understand, cope, and succeed in today's "tiger by the tail" entrepreneurial age are the genesis for *Chopstick*.

When we look at the explosive rush of seductive technology changes we see in all sectors, getting past what I call the "gee whiz" factor is often tough. And often time is of the essence—markets and technology are moving at warp speed. So on the one hand, action is needed, and on the other, you need to often drill down, be skeptical, and take a more in-depth look but at a distance.

It may surprise many, but I find the insights of Nobel Prize winning physicist Richard Feynman helpful, and I use these occasionally. Describing the role of science, Feynman notes *"… when a scientist doesn't know the answer to a problem, he is ignorant. When he has a hunch as to what the result is, he is uncertain. And when he is pretty darn sure of what the result is going to be, he is in some doubt. We have found it of paramount importance that in order to progress we must recognize the ignorance and leave room for doubt. Scientific knowledge is a body of statements of varying degrees of certainty—some most unsure, some nearly sure, none absolutely certain."*[5]

The above provides excellent counsel for management thinking when seeking to understand how business is changing, the impact of technology, and seeking rules to succeed. There are no fixed rules; keep an open mind, develop new perspectives, continuously adjust your thinking, be skeptical, seek to learn best practices of others. And recognize all assumptions must be questioned.

Dealing with today's entrepreneurial age changes demands new thinking, new ways of looking at today's changes, new perspectives, and a more nuanced, philosophical approach to understand and adapt to change. And these needs are the drivers for *Chopstick*, sharing with readers a practical, entertaining, and informative perspective about today's entrepreneurial age challenges and new ways to meet them. I do try to cover a lot of ground in *Chopstick*, moving quickly, hopefully challenging your traditional thinking. After finishing *Chopstick,* if you have gained some new ways of looking at today's challenges and opportunities, perhaps learned a few new tools, have lots of questions and more curiosity and passion for what lies ahead, then I have accomplished my mission.

Chapter 1

Entrepreneurial "Thinking": The Most Critical Survival Skill for the Twenty-first Century

All new ideas begin in a non-conforming mind that questions some tenet of the conventional wisdom.
Admiral H. G. Rickover

Perspectives on Entrepreneurial Thinking

So what is *really* needed to succeed in today's explosive global entrepreneurial business environment? How do you successfully meet the *traditional and entrepreneurial management* challenges discussed earlier? What is the magic formula? Sorry, no magic formula.

You certainly need "foundation" skills—strategy planning, marketing, financial analysis, product management, legal, and others. You need to understand, and I mean really understand, how to dissect financials, how financial P&L transactions impact balance sheets, how competitive forces reshape markets, how value chain analysis optimizes business decision making. Think of these as the basics, like premed education for a physician.

Maybe you also read the latest business best sellers, perhaps attended a top business school, and got an MBA—very helpful and impressive. And maybe you have some management experience, honed your skills to address real business challenges, and worked with strong mentors who helped sharpen your skills. Now you certainly understand the "rules" and surely have the tools, and you are ready to cope with today's explosive market morphing and business challenges.

Well, not quite. Think about it—if it was really that easy, we would see fewer business miscues and flameouts. Look at the numbers. We hear about great business successes—Google, Amazon, and many others—but the failure rate for new entrepreneurial startups is sobering; less than half survive even one year. And major firms that we assumed should know better and be here forever—NCR, General Motors, DEC, WANG, and many others—have either been gouged, dismembered or disappeared, swallowed up with ineffective management that missed a turn, fell asleep at the switch, and failed. You can be sure the management of these companies also followed the above "success blueprint" and thought they had it right, yet something went wrong.

So if you do what you are supposed to do—get the education, experience, use the so-called best practices—and yet failure rates are so threatening, what is missing here?

The missing ingredient is what I call *entrepreneurial thinking*, which I loosely define as developing new perspectives needed to understand today's challenges, where we are heading and taking new actions often "outside the box" or "outside the room" as we will discuss later. Loosely defining this new direction is no accident; in today's entrepreneurial world, definitions are less formal as is most communications. We are creating new shorthand just to talk with each other. And it is a mistake to assume there are fixed rules to deal with today's challenges; the real need is to develop perspectives, understand the changing landscape, really develop a new way of thinking.

Entrepreneurial thinking is a thread that runs throughout this book, challenging your traditional business perspectives in ways that are critical to adapt to today's entrepreneurial challenges. You may not agree with all my ideas here and should challenge and question what you read—always a good approach and what I always do. The new perspectives I share are just that—perspectives about today's changing markets, opportunities, and success strategies. Rigid rules and formal structures that remain unchallenged represent traditional thinking that is now looking like road kill as we accelerate along the global entrepreneurial highway.

Psychologists have learned that to fully develop cognitive learning skills, you must exercise the brain in ways that stimulate your less developed brain cells. Research suggests that people with stronger right brain cells may daydream and are more visual, spontaneous, and holistic in their approach to problem solving among other attributes. Overall, they are usually defined as more creative.

On the other hand, people with stronger left brain cells tend to be more methodical, detailed, structured, analytical, less visual, more logical. Recognize these are broad classifications and generalities, and most people have a mix of both left- and right-brain attributes.

Suppose we were to create a new "left brain" advanced degree program to further improve the skills of left-brain thinkers. While this would probably be helpful, it is not the best approach; it's much too narrow. Studies show offering training that drives chemical messengers across the brain's highways or synapses is the ideal way to improve overall brain function.

When you do physical exercise, the best training is to flex unused muscles. The same applies with brain cells. Training your brain to move beyond traditional thinking "comfort zones" is how you become a more effective problem solver.

Entrepreneurial thinking is a learned skill that I find achieves the above objective, helping business professionals more effectively address today's challenges and succeed. I have validated this assumption in many business situations and the classroom. No magic bullet here or get-rich-quick formula, just developing new perspectives, strategies, and different ways of looking at today's world to improve business performance, career growth, and personal satisfaction.

What I have learned in my career and experience teaching advanced business strategy and entrepreneurship courses during the past eight years honed my thinking here. Bottom line—executives able to "think entrepreneurially" are more effective, whether they are leading a two-person startup in a garage or employed by a Fortune 500 corporation. And the new thinking here goes beyond traditional business skills, such as marketing and business planning, but addresses how we communicate, deal with others across the globe, understand and manage disruptive innovation, and so on. We are talking about a new way of thinking here that, if mastered, I believe provides strong returns.

I have also found that looking backward provides good insights and markers for going forward; this is an approach I freely use in *Chopstick*. You gain great insight into what went wrong, what went right, what we can learn, and what not to do, helping create an entrepreneurial thinking blueprint. Maybe we should send this same message to our political leaders—always wise counsel learning from the lessons of the past.

Mission Statements and Entrepreneurial Thinking

A good starting point is a company's mission statement. Sounds like a boring topic to many but bear with me here. Traditional management spends considerable time and effort to precisely craft a corporate mission statement. I have been involved in many of these efforts, both helping craft mission statements for large and small organizations, as well as examining how leading firms tackle this problem. Mission statements often have a "ho-hum" reaction among staff, but these are worthwhile efforts to ensure staff is in sync, understands where the company is heading, how it will get there, what it considers important, and most important, what are its core values. Emphasizing the objective of being the lowest cost provider sends one message; emphasizing ensuring delivery of the highest quality, differentiated products sends another. Remember these not-too-subtle differences really drive corporate strategy, operational plans, and often define an organization's future success.

Mission statements also send messages about the "reach" of companies, what is their span of vision, i.e., to what extent are they looking beyond the horizon, going beyond protecting a core business vs. looking at new business models. Look at two examples; first, here is the General Motors mission statement:[6]

G.M. is a multinational corporation engaged in socially responsible operations, worldwide. It is dedicated to provide products and services of such quality that our customers will receive superior value while our employees and business partners will share in our success and our stock-holders will receive a sustained superior return on their investment."

Now here is the Google mission statement:[7]

To organize the world's information and make it universally accessible and useful.

It sure looks like Google is reaching for the stars here.

Google, founded in 1998 by two Stanford University students, started as a basic search engine, ramped up sales to about $17 billion in 2007, and achieved a market cap of about $220 billion in November 2007. Compare that to General Motors, started in 1908, led sales for seventy-seven consecutive years from 1931 to 2007, a "flagship" automobile brand, and valued at less than $20 billion in late 2007, *less than 10 _percent of Google*. Even after a $50 billion government bailout in 2009, today General Motor's market cap is only about $51 billion, *about 29 percent of Google's $173 billion*.

You can argue I selected a dramatic example here. You may also argue that Google "was in the right place at the right time," at the cusp of the Internet revolution, while General Motors is stuck in a mature business, automobile manufacturing, with nowhere to go but fight for market share in a tough, competitive global market. I consider this *traditional* thinking that really doesn't work well with markets and technologies morphing, emerging global players, and intense competition from nontraditional players.

Why Entrepreneurial Thinking Is a Critical Management Skill: Missing the Mark

Suppose in the 1990s, a GM executive made a presentation to the board of directors and shared the following vision I would have recommended related to GM's future challenges and opportunities:

- GM should expect strong competition from Japanese manufacturers.
- Given their <Japanese manufacturers> degree of manufacturing automation, we can expect significant pressure on our profit margins due to competition from Japanese manufacturers.
- Toyota's new lean manufacturing system is a new "socio-technical" system providing fully integrated manufacturing and logistics; this is a serious threat.
- We must enhance our level of automation and quality standards to compete based on both quality and cost- we need a radical "tops down" shift in how we conduct our business
- We need to expand our core business, look at ways to create new revenue streams that capitalize on new technologies and market needs. We have several directions I recommend we pursue:
    - We need to redefine the automobile business, move from producing a "product," to creating an "experience," integrating entertainment, information access, and features leveraging today's new Internet, wireless, and information technologies.
    - We have a proprietary key brand asset—OnStar—which no one else has.[8] We can build, promote, and reinforce our OnStar brand to deliver all this and more, expand well beyond its current "I need help" request function.
    - We create several benefits—we pull through new car sales; we create a new high-growth revenue streams building on next-generation services; we reposition GM as a twenty-first-century visionary company offering the

highest quality cars, integrating transportation and information technologies, and reinforcing GM's global leadership position, and send a positive signal to the marketplace.

I have no idea if the above presentation was ever made. I do know it *should* have been. Suppose the presentation *was* made, what do you think would be the reaction? The record is clear as you will see.

I have always been surprised, as mentioned earlier, how major companies with highly talented, experienced executives miss the mark and GM clearly has. I have been in similar situations many times in my career, and one in particular stands out. With several senior management consulting associates, we conducted a presentation to the board of directors of a major retailing chain. Joining me were a well-known former retailing executive now serving as a management consultant and several other highly talented senior staff. My role was typically to share a vision on how information technology was changing, where the opportunities were, and how this translated into changing business processes and business metrics, and impacted shareholder value.

Our brief but substantive presentation covered a lot of ground, looking at new retailing business models, how shareholder valuation changes with different strategy directions, projected market shifts, and so on. The reaction? Something like "Interesting, but we are focusing on our core business, which is working well. We are integrating technology within our five-year plan. We are on track and are meeting our targets comfortably. We understand the future challenges and are well positioned to meet them."

During the long ride down in the elevator, we all looked at each other but said nothing (always a good practice by the way). Outside the building, almost at the same time we said, "This management team just doesn't get it." You always want to secure new consulting engagements, but just as important you want to build relationships with management teams that understand and are receptive to new thinking, new ways to approach markets, and "best practices" honed by many other players. Our conclusion—this company was heading for trouble, and that is what happened.

I had a similar experience working as an executive in a major communications firm. Leading the effort to create a new line of business building on our core business, our team presented the business case, defining the new market opportunity, entry and growth strategies, financials, plans, and the benefits we accrue for our core business. The response? Comments such as: "This is not our core business—too risky"; "I accept this is a high-growth market, but we don't have experience in this business"; "This will divert resources from our current core business"; "We can't spend money on this—we need funds for our core business." I don't have to tell you what the board decision was on the proposed new business, and this Fortune 500 company paid a high price for not wanting to reach beyond its core business.

So let's go back to my initial question related to the GM board's reaction to the hypothetical presentation sharing a new vision for GM's future. New directions were proposed that went beyond the company's core business and probably exceeded management's experience, level of understanding, and "comfort zone." It's usually easier to say no to decisions that you don't quite grasp. And this is the *opposite* of what I view as entrepreneurial thinking, where you often have to commit resources despite *less-defined* markets, *unproven* technologies, *unknown* outcomes, and *high uncertainties*. That is why I emphasize the need for new perspectives, not rigid rules. I find this is a hard concept for traditional management to grasp, but critically needed, particularly in more traditional market sectors that are under attack today. Not surprisingly, I find students grasp this concept quickly; they have much less to "unlearn."

Important points here and we will revisit this again as we proceed through *Chopstick*.

But first let's look at a related issue—how to determine whether a new proposal is really just an idea or a real, sustainable business opportunity. There is a difference here, and it is a big one that we will discuss in chapter 2.

Chapter 2

Ideas (Even Great Ones) Are Not Opportunities

I skate to where the puck is going to be, not where it has been.
Wayne Gretzky
Canadian Ice Hockey Player

Dissecting an Idea Disguised as an Opportunity

A good starting point here, let's look at what appears to be a great opportunity but is really an *idea* for a business that needs more refinement and thinking. Drawing from several related experiences working with emerging companies, changing company and individual names, and refining some discussions to emphasize key points, I find this captures the essence of these typical discussions and provides excellent insights on the opportunity analysis process.

"Bridging the Internet to TV world, doing it smoothly, efficiently and parsimoniously is the 'Holy Grail'—we have done it with the Jupiter Model 2.0," said Fred Lindquist, Jupiter's CEO, COO, and "smart guy." Tall, lanky, thirtyish, with "one size too large" Woody Allen-like glasses, Fred was over the top excited about his new product. And Mark Frazer, Jupiter's VP of marketing, a smooth, but I guessed unseasoned recent MBA graduate, was just as excited.

Jupiter Model 2.0 plugged into the Internet and your TV. You enter your video search criteria, Jupiter finds video options, you select the desired video, and you watch it. Most are free and some you pay for, billed by Jupiter or a partner. Model 1.0 demonstrated how it works; Model 2.0 is the proposed commercial version offered to users at $10 per month. Note years ago, this looked like a breakthrough. Today, Hulu, iTunes, Amazon Video on Demand, and many other commercial services offer these services, and more are coming. But let's go back to my discussions with the Jupiter team.

"You will see we have created the next Google," said Fred. "Large-scalable market, first mover advantages, intellectual property, demonstrable prototype product, alliance partners—we have all this and more. We only need $2 million capital to meet our revenue goals of $12 million by year 2—with 80 percent of our projected revenue from subscriptions, we have a solid recurring, high-growth revenue stream here."

How my path crossed with the Jupiter team was typical—referred to me by a close friend who thought I could help focus the highly qualified technical team I was meeting here, hopefully create a fundable business, and if needed, play a senior management role, serve on the board, or support as an advisor.

I replied the business looks well positioned in a high-growth market and then proceeded to go through my usual discussion to bring this stratospheric venture back down to earth.

"What is your business focus here? Exactly what is Jupiter selling—hardware, software, content via resale, licensing technology, or are you offering a bundled service?" was my initial question directed to the CEO.

"We could do it all," said Lindquist. "We own the IP for the technology and can sell products. We see the real opportunity to offer a bundled, branded, scalable entertainment service to consumers, and that is our market entry strategy."

I always get concerned when I hear "we could do…" rather than "we will do…" It sends a signal to me that the team has lots of options, many may be good ones, but they have not fully fleshed out the details here, done the hard work needed to vet all the *ideas,* and defined the *optimum* opportunity and business strategy. The discussion proceeded.

"Why did you select this particular strategy rather than the others? Share your thinking with me on this decision," I replied.

In my experience, the response received to this question, which I always ask, provides me with a wealth of information, such as the following:

- The team's level of strategic thinking and their ability to assess, at a detailed level, the financial, market, technology, competitive, and business impact of alternative business strategies
- The tradeoffs they perceive for each of the alternative strategies, particularly for the strategies they elected *not* to pursue (a very important point)
- The extent to which technical capabilities, rather than market, competition and end user needs drive their strategic decision-making process and response
- The extent to which their proposed plan is consistent with the selected strategy
- The new management team skills that will be needed to successfully pursue the recommended business strategy (which may not be what they proposed initially)
- Their ability to understand and articulate the marketing, sales channel, and strategic alliance implications and options for each of the strategy options
- The team's perception on company value, particularly where and how value is created, how is it sustained, and what the main roadblocks are

The CEO responded saying they wanted to create a subscription-based service rather than a product business. They believed this would improve their ability to attract funding, and they also market tested the $10 subscription fee. That was the extent of the strategy planning here.

I was really asking what looked like a simple question here, and the above response provided an excellent starting point to move this to the next level. We moved on.

"I understand your strategy and model. How do you plan to use the proceeds, and explain your thinking on how the business will ramp up?" I asked, again a typical follow-up question.

"We will add four development staff to complete the Model 2.0 beta product and pilot test with a telephone carrier we are talking with," said Lindquist. "We are hiring two marketing staff and have to purchase systems and equipment—our monthly burn rate increases to $210,000 by month 6 and $2.0 million funding now will enable us to launch product by month 15 and create a scalable revenue stream." Burn rate is a standard term to define what monthly costs need to be funded.

Good response. I continued with my questions.

"Understand, now what is your thinking on sales and marketing here—who are your customers and how will you sell to them?" I asked, again a typical question.

"Well, we see building a direct to consumer marketing campaign to sign up subscribers and working with cable and telephone companies to also co-market our branded services," responded Lindquist.

"So let's see if I understand this—Jupiter offers a bundled $10 per month service, you expect to attract a minimum of one hundred thousand bundled service users by early year 2, with about 80 percent of these sold directly by Jupiter to consumers—that about right?" I asked.

We had some channel strategy issues here, but first I focused the discussion on the broader business strategy issues and tested the water for some alternatives. "Suppose I take a step back and look at this differently. Maybe to maximize opportunity here we work with *one* worldwide telephone company who may want to co-brand and globally promote the current Model 2.0 as well as accelerate a next generation Model 3.0. This strategy may offer stronger growth and higher returns for shareholders and other benefits as well. Should we explore this, and if not, why not?" I asked.

"What do you mean by 'other benefits'?" said Jupiter's CTO Mark Frazer, finally showing some interest here.

My response was long; I provided a detailed reply, saying something like this: "Well, this option creates global scale and reach, much stronger than a 'go it alone' or any limited partner strategy would provide. Co-branding with a global partner increases company value and attracts quality investors. A major partner would have incentive to support further technology development. Your intellectual property (IP) protection helps, but most know this business is moving at lightning speed and we will see other Jupiters out there offered by well-funded players. To meet market penetration objectives, you know you need to reach large scale quickly, and this strategy helps. And most important, 'going it alone' with a direct to consumer sales strategy requires significant investment, takes time, and is risky."

"Understand," said Lindquist. "I see your thinking here."

At some point in these discussions, after fleshing out the pros and cons of various strategy options, I often provide my assessment of the overall plan and how I believe it will be perceived. With the current team, I offered the following summary comments:

"I expect investors I work with will be impressed with the technical qualifications of your team—you both are obviously talented, understand the technology, have one patent pending, and also three provisional patents. Developing and executing a direct to consumer sales and marketing strategy with a subscription-based pricing structure, however, demands new management skills and a well-defined execution strategy. These really do not exist with the current strategy and plan, and investors will focus intensely on this issue. Given the pace of market growth and technology development, I believe an alternative partnering strategy should be explored, which may also include a technology licensing strategy with one or more equipment partners. Intel did quite well with a 'Powered By' strategy, and maybe that is the real opportunity for Jupiter."

Probably not exactly what the management team wanted to hear, but nonetheless that was the message I left here. So what really happened here? We started out with what looked like an *opportunity*, described to me as the "next Google," envisioning new boxes on millions of TV sets linking to the Internet, providing access to Internet-based video content generated from anywhere on the planet. After some discussion, and what I shared above are only "tip of the iceberg" points, I concluded that we really had here was an *idea* for a new business. Understanding what is an idea and what is an opportunity takes some experience and time—often not as easy as it seems, especially when seduced by new "gee-whiz" technology emerging almost daily. But there are tools and techniques that can help here.

Car Air Fresheners and Chicken Broilers

Now let's shift gears. Suppose you work for a major auto manufacturer and are asked to evaluate the potential for a new automotive-related business opportunity, maybe a new programmable air freshener device for cars. Or suppose you work in the kitchen and get an idea for a new device to more efficiently broil chickens. Obviously the chicken broiler and auto markets are different—moving roasted chickens on a spit, at first glance, has little in common with air fresheners in vehicles moving people on streets. But the initial question and basic challenges are surprisingly similar here.

The starting question for both is the same: does the idea represent a *real* business opportunity that can support a sustainable, competitive business? Even though these are very different markets and products, the tools and techniques to answer this question are actually quite similar.

Many excellent books with representative titles something like *How to Develop Business Plans, Creating Successful New Ventures,* or *How To Make Millions Creating New Products* provide roadmaps on developing new business opportunities. While the process varies, the typical approach is to flesh out and define the business into a neatly bound plan, with representative tasks as follows:

• *Summarize your mission, goals, objectives, and strategies*

Defining your mission sets the trajectory for the business and how you will operate. Strategies define your roadmap and, as mentioned before, play a key role in driving your future success. Goals and objectives define the *quantified* targets you expect to achieve.

• *Identify and quantify the market need*

Simply put, you need to understand if this is a large or niche market, who are the target buyers, what are their needs, how many do they buy today and in the future, why are existing products not meeting their needs, why is your product a better solution to meet their needs, what is willingness and ability to pay, and so on.

• *Identify the market pricing metrics and how your product fits in*

After defining product and positioning, next you need to address the pricing issues. How are competitive products priced; what are the feature/pricing tradeoffs (e.g., what is the price premium for competitive chrome chicken broilers models vs. painted models); what is your target product pricing for all models; how does your pricing for comparable "feature sets" compare to competition?

Pricing strategy is a complex subject; what I am showing here only summarizes the highlights within the business-planning process. We will revisit some of these concepts later when we discuss strategy planning in chapter 11.

- *Identify your direct and indirect costs*

What are your *direct* costs to produce your product (this enables you to define your gross margin, a key metric)? What are your *indirect* or overhead costs needed to support your operations? To develop these costs, you need to develop a sales forecast showing how many products you will sell in the initial five years after business launch. As production volumes increase, you would expect gross margins to increase due to experience and learning curve effects (i.e., the more you produce, you improve manufacturing processes and reduce your per unit costs). And overhead costs may increase as new resources may be needed to provide corporate governance, headquarters support, customer service, R&D, and similar support services. Cost for all these functions would be included in the financial plan.

- *Identify your management and staff resources*

Successful new businesses are really driven by people, not technology. Executing new business plans demands an experienced talented staff, ideally with some entrepreneurial experience. You need to ensure the "fit" is right—while you may not need staff, for example, that previously manufactured chicken broilers, a sales team with retail merchandising experience and contacts among large retail chain buyers would probably be an asset for this venture.

The above is only a summary of key business planning tasks and many resources, including entrepreneurship courses, can help. But remember our objective here—to determine whether a new business idea is a potential business opportunity. Ideas are not opportunities, and fortunes have been lost by individuals who did not understand the difference.

Creating formal, detailed business plans too early in the process I find "short circuits" the really creative thinking that is needed to define the *real* opportunity. This is a very important point here that needs repeating. **Creating a formal, neatly bound business plan that shows breakeven in eighteen months does not mean you have a real opportunity unless all options have been fully fleshed out.** The Jupiter discussion above is what I mean by the "creative thinking" process that is needed here.

Unfortunately business plans tend to have a life of their own after they are developed and printed on glossy paper with expensive binding. Business plans are often self-fulfilling prophecies—how can a plan that is so well thought out and look so good not attract smart investors and be a great success? As shown in the discussion with the Jupiter team earlier, defining the business takes some critical up-front business thinking. And this is done *before* you develop the formal business plan, or maybe spend upwards of $20,000 for support to prepare this document.

"Fingerspitzengefuhl" or Gut Feel

I have a friend in Europe who believes in the "gut feel" approach or what he calls "fingerspitzengefuhl," which loosely translated from German means "gut feel" or "feel in the fingertips." He uses this approach to determine quickly whether an idea represents a really strong potential business opportunity. Seeing many opportunities weekly, that is his approach, and it works for him and many others I am sure. For most with less talented fingertips, a more prescriptive approach is needed, a way to measure the merits of an idea and whether and how it should be pursued further.

But in today's entrepreneurial age, lengthy business plans cannot be prepared to assess good vs. marginal vs. bad vs. really bad ideas. "Gut feel," or "I think this is a great business idea" also does not work when you are spending corporate dollars to pursue new ventures. Nor does it provide comfort when you are betting a second trust on your home to create the next generation chicken broiler.

So if you don't prepare a formal business plan upfront to evaluate an idea, what do you do?

The Three-Legged Stool Model Analysis

I like to use an analysis tool called the *Three-Legged Stool*[9] model to quickly evaluate the potential and viability of new business ideas. It saves time, money, and often helps surface new ways of looking at a business—much easier to do this in a "white board" discussion rather than looking a pile of twenty-five neatly bound business plans piled on a conference room table. Here is how the process works.

Like a three-legged stool, successful ventures must have the proper balance between three elements: *opportunity, resources, and management.*

First, look at the opportunity: is what is being proposed a *significant* opportunity or *niche* business? Does this offer a scalable, defensible business model to drive high future earnings, or is this really a "lifestyle" niche business? Nothing wrong with creating a smaller "lifestyle" business—we only get in trouble when you *think* this is more than it is. That is why we go through this process.

Let's stay with the *opportunity* leg of the stool for a moment and look at our chicken broiler business. You see a major market opportunity here, believe this is a *not* a niche market, calculate you have an addressable market of maybe ten million households, after some assumptions about income and the number of people who eat broiled chicken. You have the design done, found a manufacturer, are ready to go, and are excited about the high potential opportunity here. Sounds good. It looks like we have a "high" leg stool here.

Now let's move to the *resources* leg of the stool. High potential, strong opportunities demand more, not less funding to succeed;

these resources are needed to quickly capture market share, achieve low-cost positioning, and offset competition. Otherwise risk increases and balance is impacted. Looks like we *need* a "high" leg stool here.

Finally, look at the *management* leg of the stool. You identified a major business opportunity and need a seasoned, experienced management team with diversified skills to make the operational, marketing, financial, and strategic decisions after launch to move this company forward, even with a great product. And you need a strong team to attract the *resources* needed to succeed. These are linked. Another "high" stool leg here.

So what are the implications here for our chicken broiler business *idea*? We would expect this to be a significant opportunity with strong revenue growth, require significant capital investment (ideally linked to performance milestones), and show a strong team, with diversified skills to successfully manage and grow this new venture. That is the formula, we conclude, needed here to evolve this idea to a new business opportunity. Most importantly, note this is an initial *Three-Legged Stool* model analysis—we have not even discussed the business plan, which hopefully has not yet been completed sending expensive bound copies to my desk. Going through the above analysis refines new venture thinking and is helpful based on my experience to guide business plan development.

Like a three-legged stool, we need *balance* between the three legs. The messages here? Great opportunities do not make great businesses—management and resources must be in balance. Management and resources attract like magnets to high-potential opportunities.

To further reinforce the above, consider the opportunity for creating a new upscale muffin store capitalizing on what you see is an identified need for baked goods in an exclusive New York City neighborhood. Nothing is wrong with this business—lots of people like good muffins, even better if they are *great* muffins. Maybe you can position this as a significant future franchisable opportunity, but on the surface, this looks like a "lifestyle" business. While this venture may have "shorter" opportunity, management, and resources "legs," if they are about equal, the new venture may be more manageable and perhaps more successful than a chicken broiler business.

What we have learned is new ventures that seem to have only modest potential may provide high returns. And that goes for muffin stores or Fortune 500 new business projects. This is counterintuitive. Why? Because opportunity, resources, and management *balance* may be more easily achieved with a modest business concept like a muffin store than a large-scale business idea that has one or two shorter stool legs and is *off balance*. Lots of implications here for entrepreneurs and management. So next time you say or hear the words, "this is a great opportunity, the next Google," think about whether the opportunity creates a Three-Legged Stool that is in balance and stands, maybe tips a bit, or is totally out of balance and unable to stay upright.

And of course, driving the process is innovation, fueling the emergence of new ideas. A critically essential entrepreneurial age skill, we will examine innovation from multiple perspectives in the next several chapters.

⚜

Chapter 3

Innovation Lessons I: New Product Development, Thinking "Outside of the Room"—Archimedes and the Bathtub—"Eureka!" Moments

There are two ways to study butterflies; chase them with
nets and inspect their dead bodies, or sit quietly in a
garden and watch them dance among the flowers.
Nongnuch Bassham
Readers Digest. May 2001

The Need for "Thinking Outside of the Room"

Yesterday, "thinking outside of the box" was management tool de jure. Not today. To survive today's global entrepreneurial markets, you must break the rules, go beyond the obvious, look for the unconventional to identify and scope new opportunities. Most of us know the words here and do understand this.

Look at the pace of change. Driven by Microsoft and others, we have created a massive new $7 trillion sector—computers, hardware, software, Internet, systems, support—all this happened in less than thirty years. Think about the disruption this has caused in all traditional market sectors, companies, business processes, and the careers of many.

But change goes well beyond the computer sector and is not always technology related. Remember lumberyards and local hardware stores? Home Depot and Lowe's disrupted the business model here. What about book publishing, under siege from online channels such as Amazon and others, as well as e-book and print on demand (POD) services? I can cite many examples here, but the key point is innovation is creating new business sectors, markets, processes, and companies. And depending on your situation, these arguably are positive or negative. The fact that I committed three chapters within *Chopstick* to innovation sends a clear signal on my view on its importance in fueling our entrepreneurial "rocket engine."

In chapter 3's title, you may have thought I meant "box" rather than "room." Nope. Yesterday, thinking "outside of the box" was, as said before, the management tool de jure. Break the rules; go beyond the obvious and look for the unconventional to scope opportunities. But the entrepreneurial age is moving fast, so fast, that "outside of the box" thinking just isn't good enough anymore. You must reach further, achieving what I call "outside of the room" thinking.

Most of my career has not been spent on developing new technology, but rather working with many talented staff to help me understand how it works, how to use it, what can we do with it, what are potential business models, how can it be used to make money, create business success and achieve a sustainable, defensible market position. If the technology is a true breakthrough all the better. But technology is seductive and only an enabler, a means to the end. Good counsel one should always keep in mind.

Thinking "outside of the room" often requires a creative focus on applications, not technology per se. For example, suppose a Japanese technology company creates a powerful, low-cost, unique network-based full-motion, high-definition video conferencing technology that plugs into the local Wi-Fi network. What are the target applications; how does this compare to competition; what is ideal product positioning; what are the market entry strategies; what are pricing and other financial metrics; what are the optimum distribution strategies; do we sell these through separate sales forces or through distributors? And these are "tip of the iceberg" questions.

A global satellite company wants to offer next-generation services to the health care market. What applications should they offer; how should they be positioned; what are the ideal sales channels; what are the financial metrics, and so on?

A publishing company wants to develop new services that integrate communications and information content communicating with mobile devices. Same questions here—how do we leverage the core technology to create a sustainable business?

These and many others are actual projects I and many others have addressed. And these are even more complex in the public company sector looking at earnings per share impact, impact of potential alliances, and so on.

———

We all look for ways to improve our daily lives. Suppose you really dislike going to the post office to buy stamps, so you sign up for a PC-based postage systems to create your own personal metered mail system and track postage costs. You are not inventing new technology here, just applying it, eliminating the need to buy a roll of stamps. You are also changing processes—technology is an enabler to support process change, finding new more efficient ways of accomplishing tasks and meeting objectives. This is an important point, very important. Technology is an enabler, a means to the end.

In virtually every market sector, all players really have access to similar technology. If they don't, my working "Technology Lag Rule" is they will have it in three to six months, and I find my rule is more often right than wrong. Everyone is really doing the same thing, so to speak, and quickly moving forward. Change or die is a good working rule in today's business world. Keeping a competitive edge, and in some industries just staying even, means going beyond the obvious, looking deeper, reaching out, and doing your best to assess risks and payoffs for these new directions. Finding new and more efficient ways of doing things is what progress is all about.

Market leadership demands "outside of the room" thinking and innovation—"… new ways of doing the same or new things"—is my simple definition. As the late George Steinbrenner eloquently said, "second place is the first loser" and is also not good enough given the explosive market changes we are seeing.

Sometimes when pressed for more specific examples, I reinforce the point that you really need to "push the envelope" in thinking through new applications, maybe using technology that is not yet fully developed. You can also usually be sure that if you get the applications right and show positive financial and performance metrics, the technology will follow. It always does. The explosive market demand for distance learning via the Internet for example, using voice and video, drives development of new transmission options, creative courseware, grading and management analytics, and so on—innovative technology responded well here. Many other examples can be cited here.

I have always been intrigued with the new product development process, how " thinking out of the box" techniques can be improved, why some organizations do it so well and others fail, and most importantly, how do you accelerate creative thinking and drive the "thinking out of the room" process.

Sometimes dumb luck or accidents create huge business successes—ScotchGard and Post-It Notes are products in this category.[10] There is much truth to Thomas Edison's famous quotation that I use often—"Just because something doesn't do what you planned it to do doesn't mean it's useless."

But the key question here is how does the creative process ensure innovation goes far enough, moving from "thinking out the *box*" to "thinking out of the *room*"? No easy answers here but it's interesting to look back at Archimedes in the bathtub and his "eureka moment."

Archimedes and the Bathtub: A "Eureka!" Moment

As the story goes, King Hiero commissioned a goldsmith to make a gold crown. Concerned that the goldsmith may have stolen some of the gold, King Hiero asked Archimedes to determine whether the gold crown was made of pure gold or was mixed with some cheaper metals. Archimedes was often asked to solve problems such as these for Hiero, king of Syracuse.

Pondering the problem, Archimedes took a bath and observed as he entered the bath, that water spilled over the edge. At that moment, he found the solution, got excited, jumped out of the bathtub naked, and raced home yelling, "Eureka! Eureka!" This translated to "I found the solution!" What he found was a way to precisely measure the volume of an irregular object. If you have two objects, one made of gold and one of silver or other metals, both may weigh the same, but gold is denser so the gold object's volume is smaller. So if you look at how much water each object "sends over the edge," you can determine whether the object is made of pure gold or a cheaper metal. And from that "Eureka!" moment, the Archimedes buoyancy principle evolved, which determined that for a sunken object, the volume of displaced fluid is equal to the volume of the object.

Some people do believe that bathtubs do promote creativity, and it clearly seems to have worked for Archimedes. Others prefer quiet and solitude to spark creativity, while others prefer to be highly engaged, interconnected, seeing new information through many channels to spur their creativity. What is clear, no rigid formula exists here despite a wealth of studies on how to spur creativity and "think outside the room." We all have to explore what works best for us to spur our creative juices to "think out of the room" and create our own "Eureka!" moments.

❧

Chapter 4

Innovation Frenzy: "The Researcher Spilled Liquid Fluorocarbon on Her Shoe ..."

*An important scientific innovation rarely makes its way by
gradually winning over and converting its opponents: it
rarely happens that Saul becomes Paul. What does happen
is that its opponents gradually die out and that the growing
generation is familiarized with the idea from the beginning.*
The Philosophy of Physics (1936)

Surviving Innovation Frenzy

Change is tough; just look at your own family. You may have young children. You get used to dealing with your kids at an early age. Controlled, managed, and within some limits, predictable. Overall you may feel you are doing fine—many challenges, busy juggling all that must be done, but it is working. Maybe dropping a ball or two once in a while, but under control.

Your children grow, reach the "tween" and teenage years, and get there quickly—the old rules no longer work, and you have new management, control, communications issues. You adapt and create new rules and approaches to survive these challenges. Anyone that has been there fully understands. Now you are also dealing with new people: boyfriends, girlfriends, and eventually in-laws, "out-laws," and others. Maybe you, like others, long for the "good old days" when life was simpler—we were in control, and the future, at least near term, was clearer. No more—that was yesterday.

Change is tough within families and in the business world as well. Innovation is the engine driving the entrepreneurial age "train," furiously moving today's world down the track, probably more like a rocket ship than a train, creating a frenzy touching every facet of our lives. No question, we are heading to a future, undefined world.

Whether you are trying to decide which DVD player or vacuum cleaner to buy, you have the same concerns—are you buying the next generation, "feature-rich" version or last year's model? You don't want to buy last year's model, but how do you really know? And maybe you *want* last year's model, feel that too much advanced technology and innovation is not a good thing, more sophisticated parts to breakdown, higher maintenance bills, and so on.

So let's accept the fact that innovation-driven change is messy, disruptive, and often chaotic. An innovation blueprint showing exactly what DVD player or vacuum cleaner you should buy during the next five years would be great, but impossible to create. Innovation is often unpredictable, even among the most highly skilled professionals in their respective fields. We must all adapt to survive—that is one message reinforced throughout the book. Understanding the innovation process, how it is dramatically shaping our lives, provides a powerful tool. And innovation cannot be stopped though some have tried in the past.

Innovation Drivers: Good Planning, Serendipity, or Luck?

So why do some companies manage innovation better than others? We can learn much looking at an incident that occurred at a leading chemical manufacturing firm decades ago and is captured in chapter 4's title. As the story goes, a woman researcher, while working with a new chemical compound, dropped some of the liquid on her shoes. When she used water to rinse her shoes off, the shoes repelled the water. She explored this further, and from that simple mishap, as the story goes, ScotchGard was born.[11] And the company, 3M, created a proprietary, competitive product serving millions.

Was this pure luck or serendipity? On the surface, it sure looks like 3M's success was random and unplanned, and I expect many might think so. Look a bit deeper, however, and you get a different perspective and learn a lesson or two. When I teach innovation management using the above, I always pose the question: "What do you think is the result of the accidental spill, i.e., what do you think happens next?" At 3M, researchers are *expected and encouraged* to push the envelope, make mistakes, and pursue new opportunities. 3M management reinforces this by mandating that all researchers spend at least 15 percent of their time pursuing ideas that have nothing to do with their normal tasks—pushing the envelope, looking beyond a spill to take the time to understand, research, dig deeper—all consistent with 3M's innovation management leadership position.

And 3M's commitment to innovation is reinforced in the company's mission statement:

"*To solve unsolved problems innovatively.*" Further reinforcing this commitment is 3M's impressive $1.4 billion R&D budget in 2008, about 4 percent of net sales revenue. But with these emerging new technologies, we create disruption, and the need for new business processes, the need to retool and efficiently manage production, marketing, logistics with major business segments changing every several years. And 3M does it well, an example of effective "tops down" innovation management.

I usually conclude the above example with a second question. Assume the above incident occurs at GM; what do you suppose happens next after the spill? GM and many other major firms place great emphasis on using R&D to improve efficiency in areas of manufacturing, automation processes, and materials. But history has shown, for example, GM missteps and inability to capitalize on new developments, such as electric cars, leveraging On-Star to create a major information utility, and others cited in case studies and textbooks. Given GM's profit improvement-oriented R&D emphasis, my perspective on what may happen next at GM and like-minded companies is a reprimand, maybe a "clean out your desk and a walk to the door moment." This may sound harsh, but looking at recent history, I believe this is right on target.

While not providing all the answers, understanding how innovation shapes markets, impacts traditional businesses, creates new ones, and affects every facet of our daily lives provides a good foundation to help us make sense of today's entrepreneurial age. That is also why I devoted three chapters of *Chopstick* to share perspectives on this topic.

Innovation and "Luddite" Challenges

I do sometimes meet "technology adverse" individuals who are reluctant to change. You know who they are. Maybe they don't have a smart phone, prefer to receive a letter or phone call rather than an e-mail, and when they hear the word *tweet,* think of bird calls. They view today's innovation explosion ominously as have others in past generations. Hard for many to grasp, but they do exist, with arguments like "what we are seeing is a fad, a temporary change in the market; traditional businesses will survive and return to normal; what we are seeing are market aberrations; if innovation drives technology too quickly, we will disrupt existing jobs, impact our economy, create a dire situation; and so on." Today this thinking is outdated. Newspapers are going out of business; Internet-based services provide most of what I and many others need to know. Traditional record stores are disappearing; downloadable music is displacing vinyl and CDs. No way to slow these trends down impacting all sectors and every facet of our daily lives.

But resistance to technology change is not new. During the days of the Industrial Revolution, knitting machines were introduced that displaced traditional manual workers. Opponents of progress at that time were called *Luddites,* which is defined by the *New Oxford American Dictionary* as "a member of any of the bands of English workers who destroyed machinery, especially in cotton and woolen mills, that they believed was threatening their jobs." The same citation describes a Luddite as a "person opposed to industrialization or a technology: a small-minded Luddite resisting progress."

In a recent *Smithsonian Magazine* article, Richard Conniff noted that the Luddite legend started with Ned Ludd, also known as Captain, General, or even King Ludd, who first turned up as part of a Nottingham protest in November 1811 and was soon on the move from one industrial center to the next. This elusive leader clearly inspired the protesters, and his apparent command of unseen armies, drilling by night, also spooked the forces of law and order. Government agents made finding him a consuming goal.

In fact, as Conniff notes, no such person existed. Ludd was a fiction concocted from an incident that supposedly had taken place twenty-two years earlier in the city of Leicester. According to the story, a young apprentice named Ludd or Ludham was working at a stocking frame when a superior admonished him for knitting too loosely. Ordered to "square his needles," the enraged apprentice instead grabbed a hammer and flattened the entire mechanism. The story eventually made its way to Nottingham, where protesters turned Ned Ludd into their symbolic leader.[12]

Today's "Luddite challenge" is to educate traditional business managers on how technology change will disrupt both traditional business processes and business models. I chose the words carefully here. We all know technology can improve processes, create efficiencies, and so on. But disruption is different, cutting to the core of the business, changing business models, forcing staff to "think out of the room," leaving their comfort zone. Let's look at some leaders and losers in the innovation process—there are some lessons to be learned here.

Learning from a Leader in the Innovation Process

Let's first look at an innovation leader, Microsoft Corporation.

Look at Microsoft today, reporting a drop of 17 percent in third quarter 2009 revenue due to a severe market drop in PC sales. PC sales pull through sale of Microsoft software products, so the drop is both defensible and understandable. But the same announcement also noted that the sales drop was due to "increased competition from network based software services"—these directly compete with Microsoft Office and other "boxed" software product sales. What does this mean?

Looking beyond the words and numbers here, most know that in today's entrepreneurial age, the Internet will serve as the primary distribution channel for software and entertainment products. It may be hard for some to grasp now, but most future software will either be downloaded to your PC, or you will pay to use on the Internet. That is the concept of today's "cloud computing" trends now being embraced by many existing players. And many new entrepreneurial age startups are entering this embryonic, high-growth market.

So back to our Microsoft example, what are the implications here? Google is now offering network-based word processing, spreadsheet, and related programs encroaching on Microsoft's market. The Apple iPad offers Apple-branded word processing and spreadsheet programs that will capture market share. We are creating a new software market business model. So two key questions emerge here:

- What is the outlook for Microsoft's "boxed" software business now being sold in stores? The real issue here is what happens to this traditional Microsoft growth market. Does Microsoft add more enhancements, invest in further innovation to protect its core business? Or does Microsoft "jump" to a new line of business and offer network-based software, maybe a "cloud-based" version of Word and Excel?[13]

- Assuming Microsoft "jumps" to a new line of business, the network-based software business, how does Microsoft handle this disruptive innovation? Think about the impact on major retailers such as Best Buy with racks of boxed Microsoft software products that will now be available via download with a few clicks and a credit card. What about the revenue and earnings impact for Microsoft? Ramping up the new network-based business will take time and money and create market excitement, but will impact earnings unless carefully managed. On the positive side, Microsoft's entry into the network-based software market will also drive sales of Microsoft's new network-based "Bing" search engine designed to compete with Google's main business. Disruptive innovation usually closes some doors, but often opens new ones.

While it is too early to yet see how the Microsoft market will evolve, we can expect this market leader to understand and capitalize on today's rapidly changing software services market.

Learning from Losers in the Innovation Process

I find great value and often learn lessons by looking back, what mistakes were made, what worked, what didn't, and what we learned. This is a powerful learning technique used within analysis of case studies develop by Harvard Business School and others. Let's start with NCR, the cash register company.

NCR started as the National Manufacturing Company of Dayton, Ohio, and is credited with manufacturing and selling the first mechanical cash register, invented in 1879 by James Ritty. In 1884, the company and patents were bought by the Patterson brothers, John Henry and Frank, and they renamed the company the National Cash Register Company. The Patterson brothers formed NCR into one of the first modern American companies, introducing aggressive sales methods and business techniques.[14]

Fast forward to 1967. NCR had built a leadership position in the mechanical cash register business, offering all the features customers wanted. And NCR had built a superb, highly efficient production and support "machine" to design, manufacture, sell, and support mechanical cash registers. But computer technology was on the horizon, so what should NCR do? They needed to protect their business, enhance their current products with features customers want, meet customer needs—this meant funding enhanced "mechanical" cash registers. Yet they knew computers would eventually impact their business—when and by how much were the questions. NCR's vice president for finance at the time, J.J. Hangen, took a "stick to the knitting approach," telling the press, "The base of NCR's revenue comes from <electro mechanical> cash registers and accounting machines. Computers both support and *protect* NCR's traditional product line."[15]

Thinking that the next technology wave is coming to *protect* and not *displace* your products did not work four decades ago and does not work in today's entrepreneurial age. Within seven years, NCR's core business, electromechanical cash registers, slipped from 90 percent of the market to about 10 percent replaced by computers, obviously turning the company upside down. Disruptive technology impacts many companies.

Imagine you are a Kodak executive, you built a career selling film products, offering a range of competitive "100, 200, 800" speed products—high quality, best in the market—you understand your business and have done well here. Now digital cameras emerge. Quality was not great at the start, but improving quickly. Looks like it will never catch on for "serious" photographers. We all know the history here. Traditional film has all but disappeared in almost all photographic market segments. How Kodak managed this transition, resisting the film to digital movement, is the subject of several excellent Harvard Business School and other case studies.[16]

Innovation: Four Key Lessons

Take a step back from the above, and we can learn four lessons here.

First markets change, always. Changes are driven by technology innovation, and they occur in every sector. It makes no difference; whether you are in the transport business, cleaning services, book publishing, restaurant business, or sell shoes, you can be sure that technology changes will impact your business, change your business model, create (or sometimes eliminate) competition, and often reshape total industries. Guaranteed.

Second, understanding how these changes occur, what they mean, and developing the perspectives and tools to respond to these changes ensures both survival and career growth. New perspectives are particularly critical here.

Third, and this is most important, technology innovation is a means to an end, a tool to achieve new applications, tools, services, and solutions, a driver for new business. Saying this another way, new technology success demands innovative business models that demonstrate business viability—that is a key test that must be met. And these models are often disruptive, radically so. Sometimes reshaping existing business or creating new ones as we will see with Intel later in this chapter. Technology must also move beyond what I call the "gee-whiz" factor—drill down is needed to fully grasp its impact.

Finally, if you have gained business experience, maybe were fortunate enough to have worked as a management consultant or have been a student of management, you quickly realize that basic rules of innovation management do exist and can be learned. Innovation must look beyond the obvious, like Archimedes watching bathwater overflow and creating the Archimedes buoyancy principle, "thinking out of the room" (or bathtub in his case) to create a "Eureka!" moment.

Let's look further into the innovation process, innovation management tools, and winners and losers in the innovation process.

⚬⚭⚬

Chapter 5

Perspectives on the Innovation Process: Going up the "Innovation Staircase" without Tripping

No sensible decision can be made any longer without taking into account not only the world as it is, but the world as it will be.
Isaac Asimov

What Is the Innovation Process?

So what exactly is the innovation process, how is it measured and managed, who really does it well and why, and what can we learn here?

As a starting point, we need an example of an innovative product and a framework to dissect the innovation process.

Suppose for the hypothetical new product, we again use the next generation video device "Jupiter Model 2.0" discussed in chapter 2. The product links to the Internet and enables you to select and instantly download any movie from any Internet source on the planet. Sounds like I am reaching far out for this example. Not really—as mentioned earlier, many services now offer similar features. If you are in the movie rental business or a filmmaker trying to preserve royalty revenues, think about the changes you can expect driven by this technology innovation. Back to our example, the entry level Jupiter Model 2.0.

Next, we use the S curve, a deceptively simple, easy to understand model to explain the innovation process. This is the traditional tool used by many to analyze innovation and show how innovation drives product evolution. Studied by academic scholars, used by management professionals, taught in business schools, S curve "thinking" drives and helps manage innovation, showing a roadmap for the life of a product or service, what enhancements are planned over time.

I often use the S curve to explain innovation issues and management techniques. Think of a graph—the vertical access is value or benefit to a customer; the horizontal axis is time increasing to the right. The final graph will, as you will see, be in the shape of the letter *s*. Now let's look at the evolution of the Jupiter Model 2.0 product.

After the model is built and test marketed, we put a dot in the lower area of the graph. Based on the market test, we add some new features before starting a full national sales campaign—add another dot slightly higher and to the right showing more benefits over time. Connect these initial dots; the slightly upward pointing, relatively flat line is called the entry stage of the S curve.

The Jupiter engineers further refine and enhance the Jupiter Model 2.0 product—add more dots higher and to the right. Now product sales ramp up, customers adopt the Jupiter Model 2.0, the press writes about it, the company accelerates production, and the Jupiter may even serve as the industry de facto standard. With sales soaring, management understands that R&D drives innovation and innovation increases customer value and sales. So Jupiter increases R&D investment and adds more new features, which help offset possible new competition. Add more dots ramping up to the right. Business is good; connect the dots and the line drawn, probably at a forty-five-degree angle or so, is called the "growth" phase of the S curve.

Management is encouraged by Jupiter Model 2.0 growth, keeps adding value, more features, and more "dots" hoping to show increased customer value. But after connecting the dots, the benefit and user value for the Jupiter Model 2.0 flattens out despite the new investment. Why can't we just keep adding features and increasing sales and value here?

Many forces may account for the flattening called the "maturity" phase of the S curve. New competition emerges offering the same features at lower cost. Maybe users do not want the features offered, but want new features missed by management—the "wrong bells and whistles" problem. Or maybe the standalone video player market, even with the ability to watch any film on the planet, is really just a fad market after all (remember eight track audio tapes), with the same capability offered as an optional feature within new TVs. TiVo, as an example, dramatically flattened the market for standalone DVD devices.[17] Each of these factors has the same impact; they flatten the S curve and send a clear signal to management—no more growth with Jupiter Model 2.0 product without some major retooling and repositioning.

What happened here? Let's take a step back. Innovation created a new market driven by a new product, the Jupiter Model 2.0. Innovation helped develop and grow the market with new features; competition is now using the same innovation-driven strategy to create the next S curve, advance technology to the next plateau, raise the bar, forcing all players, including Jupiter, to spend more on R&D to stay in the game. And we see Jupiter, the company that forged the new market, now scrambles to survive. And remember this new market disrupted the movie rental market, forcing traditional movie rental players to look at how the Jupiter Model 2.0 may impact their respective S curve, and often business survival.

Going up the "Innovation Staircase" without Tripping

Several years ago, I developed the Staircase Innovation Model or SIM to help explain to entrepreneurs, investors, and students innovation theories and strategies, moving from abstract concepts to a simpler entrepreneurial age, action-oriented tool.

Similar to the S curve model, the SIM concept views the S curve as a staircase. The lower landing is the entry stage; the upper landing is the maturity stage of the product, and the steps are the growth phase. It is deceptively simple model to explain, and useful to help understand innovation and market forces at work, and how they interact.

Today's entrepreneurial age frenzy is stressing the innovation process, tearing up and restructuring markets. Using the SIM concept, we can gain insights on innovation's impact. Consider the following observations:

- All companies typically go up the innovation "staircase," but some do it faster than others; some also have staircases with small baby steps; others have large ones.
- To promote innovation, companies should promote the innovation staircase among their employees to develop new products and enhance old ones; some companies do this well, others not so well.
- Companies need to understand what drives them up the innovation staircase to ensure they know if they are making real, sustainable progress.
- Companies need to constantly evaluate whether it is time to leave the current staircase and jump to a new one.
- Companies need to understand when they do jump to a new staircase, which one will be the main staircase driving growth. Will it be the new or the existing staircase?

Missing a New Innovation Staircase: The NCR Story

Let's go back to the NCR case. What went wrong, and what could have been done better? NCR went up their "electromechanical cash register staircase." They started at the lower landing, added a new feature, and took a step—added another feature customers wanted and took another step. It's always a good idea to listen to customers, or so they thought. And they kept going to invest and improve quality.

The mistake NCR and others often make is believing computer technology is helping them move up their staircase faster or take larger steps—fallacious thinking and the downfall of many companies. No, emerging computer technology in this example *really represented another staircase*, with products serving the same market, with both improved capabilities and cost performance. That is really what is meant by disruptive innovation—not here to protect you, but *disrupt* your traditional ways of doing business, challenging all industry players in all market sectors to change their thinking, employ an entrepreneurial age mindset or die, figuratively speaking.

Remember it is always easier and less risky to keep doing business as usual, not rock the boat, stay on the current staircase in most businesses. Wrong decision for NCR.

Innovation Success Story: W. L. Gore & Associates

Let's look at another company example I often use, W. L. Gore & Associates, to show how innovation can completely transform a company. In 1958, William L. ("Bill") and Genevieve ("Vieve") Gore launched W. L. Gore & Associates. Started in 1958 in the basement of their home in Newark, Delaware, Bill Gore left his job at Dupont to pursue his belief in the untapped potential of the polymer PTFE (technically, polytetrafluoroethylene). Initially W. L. Gore developed an insulated wire and ribbon cable for defense and computer applications and created a substantial business, even providing cables used on the NASA's Apollo 11 lunar landing module in 1969.

In 1969, Bill Gore stretched PTFE as rapidly as possible. Instead of breaking as expected, the stretched PTFE was strong, highly porous, and versatile. And that is how the windproof, breathable fabric Gore-Tex was created, used in a wide range of products.[18, 19]

But W. L. Gore continued to be an innovation leader, developing guitar strings using a modified polymer to create a coated string providing a coating over the entire string which stops foreign objects from getting into the winding. Today, W. L. Gore's Elixir Strings brand retains a major share of the guitar string market.

So was the above success the result of luck, skill, or good planning? You may conclude that Gore-Tex was stumbled upon while pursuing other R&D projects, and let's not forget serendipity. Sometimes things just happen, both good and bad. In this case, good things.

My experience looking at many of these situations and also being directly involved in quite a few is that many factors play a role—luck, serendipity, management, and competence. But look closely at firms like Google, 3M, and others that create a climate supporting innovation and craft mission statements that send the right signals to employees. Coupled with innovation incentives, these firms have the optimum strategy to capitalize on innovation in today's entrepreneurial age. And that also means when a researcher spills some unknown liquid on the floor and it seems to have unique features, she should not be asked to clean out her desk and be walked to the door. Maybe a better idea is to first determine what happened, what are the possibilities, what are possible ways we can use this. That should be the thinking of today's entrepreneurial age innovation leaders.

Innovation in Practice: Intel's Successful Approach

Consider the management philosophy of Andrew Grove, founder and former chairman and CEO of Intel and whom I and many others consider a leader in entrepreneurial thinking. Grove sent a clear message on his philosophy. Understand where markets and technology are going and take whatever action is needed. Period.

Going back to my innovation staircase analogy, Intel is an excellent example of a company not afraid to jump to a new staircase (i.e., new line of business) while plenty of steps are still left in their current staircase. The analogy may sound a bit precarious, but it is not. Remember each staircase may represent a company's line of business—say mechanical cash registers for NCR. The strategy question facing NCR was do they continue up the mechanical cash register staircase and use technology to maybe take bigger steps, maybe go faster but stay on the same staircase. Or should they jump to a *new* landing and start a new "computer terminal" staircase.

Compare Intel to NCR, Xerox, and many other companies and you see that the last point—the willingness to jump to a new staircase—takes courage. And that is often what separates winners from losers in today's entrepreneurial age driven market morphing. Staying the course, using yesterday's technology in today's explosive global entrepreneurial market is a recipe for failure.

Understanding how to navigate between taking steps, baby steps or big ones, on your innovation staircase, and when to "jump" to a new staircase addressing both current and new markets is the challenge that, in today's entrepreneurial age, separates the winners from the losers.

∘🗤∘

Chapter 6

Worm on a Chopstick: The Challenge of Animal and Food Boundaries—Lessons for Global "Road Warriors"

Worms seem to be the great promoters of vegetation, perforating and loosening the soil, rendering it pervious to rains and the fibers of plants by drawing straws and stalks of leaves and twigs into it; and most of all, by throwing up such infinite numbers of lumps of earth called worm casts, which being their excrement, is a fine manure for grain and grass. The earth without worms would soon become cold, hard-bound, and void of fermentation and consequently sterile.
Charles Darwin

Global Road Warrior Challenges

Working in the international business arena for several decades seasons you. Global business is tough—make no mistake about it. But that view is not shared by all. Students I find have a perspective that the global market has a mystique and is exciting. Many want to pursue international positions. And many students I have worked with have international backgrounds and are comfortable working within diverse cultural environments.

Business professionals, particularly those early in their career, also see the excitement and opportunity in the global business world.

The global business environment is exciting and challenging. But it is also helpful to add a dose of reality here, maybe temper some of the excitement here, maybe present a more realistic view of the challenges faced by global road warriors. After all, to make global business happen, you need people to travel the globe and conduct business. These global "road warriors" are what we will be talking about here. I expect after reading this chapter, most will have a more balanced perspective on the global business mystique, meaning there may be excitement and benefits, but it is also tough and demanding.

Years ago, my work with an international company based in New York City required that I often meet with overseas partners primarily in Europe and Asia Pacific. Having small children at the time, I kept my trips short and tightly planned—weekends were important as parents of small children know well. While I traveled extensively to the Asia Pacific region, for example, I can count on hand (really just a few fingers) the number of weekends I missed at home during a decade of work with this international firm. So how did I do it?

With management responsibilities at headquarters, I often was in my New York City office Monday morning. Late Monday, I may have caught a plane to Brussels, a good starting point in Europe. I was also able to sleep on plane trips, which does help.

Arriving early Tuesday morning, I would typically shower and change at an airport mini-hotel room, maybe nap for an hour, and meet with our partner's senior management at about 10:00 a.m.. And after coffee, maybe some sherry, business discussions would proceed working through lunch. Keep in mind the sherry aperitif, the wine before and during lunch and possibly a creamy fish or steak dish were all consumed with your body clock saying something like *"… it's only 5:00 a.m.—I should be having coffee, maybe eating cereal and a muffin."* After our meal, I would depart for the train station and may catch a train to Paris, arriving late in the day, checking into a Paris hotel. Typically I would schedule a dinner meeting with our local partner's management team.

On Wednesday morning, discussions with the Paris partner would conclude, and I would head to the airport to catch a plane to London. Arriving in London late Wednesday afternoon, I would check-in to the London hotel and schedule dinner with our local partner's senior management team. Early Thursday morning, discussions would conclude, and I would catch an early flight back to New York City. Taking advantage of the five-hour time difference, after arriving, I sometimes caught a taxi back to my New York office arriving late Thursday. Or after landing I would go home, often arriving at my usual time, just as if I commuted from my New York City office that day.

I may repeat the above every three to four weeks, usually targeting different countries, sometimes squeezing one more country into my European schedule. But I did try to stay in a similar overall time window. Working for another international company, I once stayed overnight in Oslo, Norway, and had a breakfast meeting with a local partner. After breakfast, I caught a plane to Copenhagen for a meeting with a partner and other principals at an airport conference room. After the meeting, which ended late morning, I caught a plane to Madrid, to attend a formal luncheon with our local partner's senior management team. After the lunch, which lasted several hours, I was whisked to the airport to catch a plane to London for a planned dinner meeting. I recall sitting at the dinner meeting and thinking that I had breakfast that day in Oslo and had made a few stops along the way before arriving in London.

Couple the above with an occasional trip to Japan, Australia, Singapore, and other Asia Pacific points and you see the challenges here. Many others have similar and even more daunting road warrior challenges given the explosive global drivers fueling today's entrepreneurial age.

On the Sunday before embarking on a planned trip like the above, I would often get together with friends and talk about what our upcoming week looks like. Some friends were "staying local"; others may have had a business trip to Boston, Chicago, San Francisco, or other places. When they turned to me, I always did my best to downplay what I did, usually saying something like "I have a few meetings in Europe this week—visiting Paris, Brussels, and London and be back the end of the week." I downplayed this because I knew the reactions, which were usually comments like this, particularly from new friends: "Wow, you are going to Paris, my favorite city—wish I had a job like that," or "Great you can see the world, visit all these exciting global places I only read about." And other similar comments.

And that is the perception here—the glamorous world of the global "road warrior."

But perception is not reality. Look at the above schedule—not much time in there for a city tour or to see a museum. Sure, you may eat well, maybe dining in the finest restaurants, traveling as a guest hosted by a senior management partner. The above is a tough travel schedule, however; keep in mind your body clock is also twisted. We are talking about a five-hour time difference for travel within Europe. And when attending meetings in Japan, drinking Sake at dinner, you do want to forget that your body thinks it is 6:00 a.m. and breakfast time.

So why not stretch these trips out, take more time, arrive on Saturday, harmonize with the local time zone, see the sites, and enjoy yourself? Sure seems like a much better approach. It is and some do. But remember, most of us have other responsibilities to manage. Maybe you have headquarters staff to manage or important meetings to attend. And what about your son or daughter's softball game? It sure would be nice to show up here. Paris in the springtime may be a nice place to visit, but your family also expects you to show up at softball games, dance recitals, or just "be there."

Going beyond the business and strategic challenges facing global road warriors in today's interconnected global entrepreneurial marketplace, balancing personal and business demands is a tough, demanding hurdle to cross. And what I shared above is typical at least for the many international senior management staff I have worked with. Fast trips. Complete your business and return to manage your other responsibilities. And take a vacation, maybe use free airline award tickets to visit these places.

My experience is when I share the above, and after providing more insights into how global business works (chapter 13), I usually temper perspectives on the global business mystique. Sure, it is exciting, and you do meet diverse, interesting people (most of the time fortunately); nonetheless, it is both challenging and demanding on both families and individuals. This sobering is a good thing. I find adding a dose of reality is always helpful.

After going through the above and sharing other global business perspectives, I do expect to see a more realistic understanding of the global road warriors' challenges and what is needed to succeed in this world. If I do not see this response, I like to share my "Worm on a Chopstick" story, which I find is an excellent learning tool and also the title of *Chopstick*. This incident happened early in my career years ago. Since that time, for those that have any doubt after reading this, I really have learned to enjoy some sushi dishes and other Japanese food. Really. I also should again emphasize names and locations have been changed here as well as throughout *Chopstick*.

And for those wondering, yes, this really happened.

When using this as a learning tool in classes, I also call it the "Incident at the Sho-Ree Palace" mentioning the fictitious name of a Tokyo restaurant. The story goes like this:

Incident at the Sho-Ree Palace

Subterranean and dark, the Sho-Ree Palace is like many traditional dinner clubs in Tokyo. Below street level near the Ginza, Tokyo's upscale luxury shopping district, the Sho-Ree's motif is crimson and purple, black as night, maybe a bit too dark for my taste. Having "survived" many previous dinners with senior management executives in Japan, I was ready to take another "notch in my chopsticks" for the dinner that lay ahead.

Japanese food is not for the meek. Many Americans say they like Japanese food, often mentioning shrimp tempura or beef teriyaki as their favorite dish and sushi is popular. But go to the Sho-Ree or other Tokyo dinner houses, and you encounter more native Japanese foods, most of which have seen little flame, often stare back at you and, in some of the most highly rated restaurants, move, sending a clear signal on just how fresh it is. These uncooked delicacies—combinations of raw fish, seaweed and various undefined sea creatures—that is what *I* mean when I say Japanese food.

Dr. Koji, president of Cozee Electronics, our host, led the way down the narrow, dimly lit circular, chiseled stone steps into the depths of the Sho-Ree, followed closely by Mr. Innatti, Cozee's head of international relations. After a successful day of meetings, a long day working through translators, and endless circular negotiations, tonight's dinner was traditional to further bond an expanding business relationship.

That Japan spends more per capita on business entertainment surprises no one who does business here. The interaction in these after-hour dinners is always more important than the day's work. Keep in mind that unless you have the stature of former President George H.W. Bush, you must also "keep your food to yourself" or risk great embarrassment and "loss of face."

Thus successful business dealings in Japan demand a delicate balance. On the one hand, you need to ensure you show professionalism, politeness, and graciousness—the Japanese are gracious and outstanding hosts. On the other hand, you must meet the daunting food challenge; as President Bush learned, this can be difficult. And that was nothing compared to the unfolding events at the Sho-Ree.

We removed our shoes, carefully placing them on a neatly pressed bamboo mat near an exquisite oriental vase, detailed with dragons and distinctive pearl beading. Sliding bamboo and silk doors revealed Dr. Koji's reserved table, neatly set with traditional black lacquered plates, engraved plastic chopsticks, and porcelain soup spoons with an intricate blue design. Japanese table settings radiate color, harmony, and formality.

"Campi," said Dr. Koji, inviting us to join him in a toast drinking Sake, Japan's traditional rice wine. After an initial round of Chivas Regal, we focused on our first dish, a too-thick slice of raw squid, shrimp, and some noodles on a lettuce bed. Long ago mastering the art of chopsticks, I picked and poked the squid, doing my best to squish it, press it, mush it, and try to make it into what I thought would be more edible. More Chivas Regal—it did help at times like this. But things quickly got worse.

I guess I saw him after the second drink, slowly slinking up my engraved, plastic chopstick emerging from the noodles. A long slim worm, clearly uncooked (he was in good company on that point), in the wrong place at the wrong time for both of us. As a young, but somewhat seasoned international veteran, many thoughts go through your head at moments like this, even after two drinks.

First, was he supposed to be there? Maybe he was part of the meal and added as a condiment, like adding an olive to a salad. Maybe added at the request of our host as an act of hospitality for his distinguished U.S. guest. Food freshness is highly valued in Japan, but this is going too far; food is not supposed to move in the plate or, for that matter, go up your chopstick. At least I didn't think so.

Maybe he was symbolic and revered in Japan and should not to be eaten or hurt, but just stick around and go where he wanted. I also knew this critter had been around for 120 million years, a lot longer than us, and in the time of the Egyptian Pharaohs, Cleopatra said worms were sacred. Maybe I was reaching here, but didn't know for sure. Traditions were important here, and I need to be respectful as a guest.

No, after careful consideration of the above, I made the instant decision this guy was not supposed to be in my plate. Next decision, what do you do? I went through my options. I could jump back, shout, and complain about sanitary food preparation; that may work in a U.S. restaurant, but do this in Japan and you will go down in a ball of flames. Or I could quietly tell my host there was a problem with my food—I seemed to be sharing it with an uninvited guest. Great embarrassment from which it is hard to recover. It may not seem like much of a problem to most people here, but it is in Japan. Wrong approach in a culture that prides itself on pleasing guests and doing proper things properly. More Chivas Regal.

I formulated a plan my experience suggested would work and ensure no embarrassment. I continued talking with my hosts, calling no attention to my unwelcome guest, who was now making great progress climbing up my chopstick. I discretely took the chopstick and tapped it one the table, trying to throw the visitor onto the table. One tap, two taps—this guy wouldn't budge, and I was thinking he is glued on, maybe with some ancient substance he secreted. Finally I shook him free, while I continued to discuss with my hosts how the global information industry was evolving. Quietly I took my napkin and crunched the visitor on the table, a very loud crunch, I thought, given his size. Dipping the chopsticks in the Chivas Regal, for sanitizing purposes now, dinner continued uneventfully with face saved and relationships preserved. More Chivas Regal and another "notch in my chopsticks."

I use the above story to share many messages. There is a need to understand other cultures whose values and ways of conducting business differ from ours. Often the ability to both understand and respect these cultural differences is the critical factor to achieve success in the global business arena. And what that means, as suggested above, is the need to understand how to balance your own cultural needs and your ways of doing business with the needs of others. And this is dynamic, often demanding that you watch what words you use, what body gestures you show, and of course, how you handle the issue of an unwelcome guest traveling up your chopstick.

There are other lighter messages in the above story, such as never eat food that moves and disinfectant applications for Chivas Regal. To this day, I still wonder if the critter was really supposed to be there. Maybe Cleopatra and the Pharaohs had it right. I may have destroyed the ultimate, sacred delicacy without even realizing it.

❦

Chapter 7

Long Tail Marketing: Selling Less of More to Make More (Dollars)

*Strategy and timing are the Himalayas of
marketing. Everything else is the Catskills.*
Al Ries

The 80/20 Rule

To understand the long tail marketing phenomenon, a good starting point is the "80/20" rule.

Most readers understand the 80/20 rule, often widely used to make a single point; in most companies 20 percent of customers generate 80 percent of sales.

First coined by Vilfredo Pareto, an early 1900s Italian philosopher, the 80/20 rule or "Pareto Principle" derived from observing that "…eighty percent of Italian land was owned by twenty percent of the population." From that starting point, the 80/20 rule institutionalized in our business culture.

The numbers may vary, but the point is the same. A small group of relatively few customers generate the bulk of revenues and often profits. Do a good job addressing the core group of most valuable customers and you win. Spend too much time on the smaller, less profitable customers, the "20 percent," and you lose. If you have retail store, you devote your costly shelf space to display those items that generate the bulk, 80 percent or more of your profits. That is the 80/20 rule in action.

If you have high-volume customers, you ensure they are well supported. If 80 percent of sales are via major retailers, and 20 percent direct to consumers, you may employ dedicated support staff for major retailers and provide consumers with an 800 number talking to a machine.

The above traditional strategy is quickly being reshaped by today's "long tail" marketing revolution.

How Today's Long Tail Marketing Revolution Is Changing the Game

Blockbuster, started in 1985, was the largest DVD and video game rental company on the planet. The top one hundred movies accounted for about 70 percent of Blockbuster's sales. By contrast, for Netflix, the largest Internet-based DVD and video game rental company, the top movies only represent 40 percent of sales with their major revenue coming from rentals of less well-known, second- and third-tier movies. These numbers are rapidly changing as the video service market morphs.

All players are moving to expand their model, but these numbers emphasize their respective core strategy. Many of today's major players, in all sectors, are now exploring how they can *slide down the tail*, a new term addressing the need to focus more precisely on many narrow market segments. NETFLIX has done this well.

And many more Amazon and Netflix's are on the horizon, using new Internet-based marketing tools to sell small numbers of a large variety of products. Look at a traditional sales generation tool. Mailing millions of pieces of "dead tree" packages (i.e., "mail") to millions of people, getting 3 percent to respond, and calling that a success is traditional thinking. That will change quickly given today's Internet, social media-driven environment.

Traditional media and entertainment sectors are also morphing, driven by the infinite number of options. Traditionally, you went to movie theaters to see the latest blockbuster. You bought CDs to hear the latest popular group. And you went to Blockbuster anxiously awaiting the DVD release of a new movie.

None of the existing sectors will go away, but they will continue to be under intense pressure. The tsunami that we see now is the "infinite shelf space" concept, the notion that all items can be displayed and, if you sell enough "onesies and twosies," you can create a profitable business.[20] That is the Amazon model and being pursued by others in all sectors seeking to "slide down the tail."

Obviously the Internet played a role here. But one of today's most powerful long tail marketing drivers, social media, I find is not well understood, but given its impact today and where it is heading, it should be. Social media is a force driving the long tail marketing phenomena. Let's take a closer look at this exciting area.

Social Media and the "New Influencers"

The social media revolution is a relatively new force reshaping traditional business models, changing the way we market, produce, and support products and services. Surprisingly, I find many senior executives have been slow to understand and internalize the new social media issues and opportunities. And if properly employed, emerging firms can often level the playing field, looking like a much more established firm than they are.

Social media, what most typically know as blogs, Facebook, and a wide array of other sites and services, are driving new entrepreneurial marketing, offering new tools to address 80/20 long tail opportunities. Social media and its impact deserve more discussion than space permits in *Chopstick*—this should be a separate book given its relevance. But I do feel I should address how social media is helping drive today's entrepreneurial thinking.

One significant new direction is the relatively new concept of *New Influencers*, individuals who reshape and channel other information.[21] New social media drives creative ways to dialogue with both customers and all players within an organization's community of interest. New terms, such as *conversational marketing*,[22] are emerging to describe how social media helps create strong dialogue with customers, building a mutual level of trust that can, if properly managed, improve business results. The dialogue cuts across all business functions—advertising, sales, customer support, and even R&D where social media feedback can be used to shape product developments.

When you read the above, to really understand the scope of change here, keep in mind traditional thinking. Say you want to reach a washing machine manufacturer. You have an 800 number, maybe go through endless voice prompts, maybe and more likely not reach a real human being. Maybe you want to discuss service options, possible accessories, or understand what new models are coming. Taking a step back, you see this is a highly inefficient process. It wastes time, frustrates customers, and increases costs with no real benefit.

Often not much better if you visit the company's Web site, navigating through great graphics, perhaps a video or two, maybe even play a game. If after all this your questions are still not answered, then an e-mail prompt appears, and you can send an e-mail to support@greatwashingmachinecompany.com or some other nondescript address. No human being is mentioned; you are part of the "80" here, the masses and handled as such, and talk to "support" whoever that is. We can all relate to this—every sector and virtually all companies. This is yesterday's traditional thinking, which is now changing quickly, driven largely by new social media and the 80/20 long tail marketing trends.

Advertising Sector: Traditional vs. New Directions

I find one good starting point in long tail marketing discussions is to look at the advertising sector; their traditional driver is to reach *mass* audiences. Emphasis here is on the "80" rather than the "20." Newspapers, television, and other mass advertising talk about targeting "the masses" and with hit rates of 3 percent or so often defined as success. Not good enough given the powerful new social media tools, techniques, and analytics that are here today and rapidly improving.

Large sums of money are spent on network advertising to reach a targeted group of potential buyers. Advertising, whether network TV, billboard, magazine or Web based, is driven by *gross rating points* (GRPs).

Simply defined, GRP measures the size of an audience viewing an ad of any type. So if an ad reaches 5 percent of an audience and the ad is repeated three times, this provides a GRP of fifteen points. In the network TV advertising business, for example, major companies plan their advertising budgets purchasing a total GRP to reach their target customers while minimizing purchase costs.

GRP also really measures reach and penetration, not costs. Costs are addressed by other metrics such as *cost per thousand* (CPM), the cost to reach one thousand people or households. Similarly *cost per point* (CPP) is the cost to reach 1 percent of a company's potential target audience. Not a perfect system and does have flaws. After all, in the network TV business, exposures to an ad does not mean people *actually* watched it—maybe they got up and had a sandwich or changed channels during the commercial. Nor does it measure how the channel used is perceived by the targeted audience; obviously credibility of the messenger, the program in this case, plays a role in the buying decision.

This is the traditional advertising model used for decades. Just like newspapers will never disappear but coexist with other media, today's advertising model is under pressure and will evolve. And this will happen faster given the explosive growth of social media. A more entrepreneurial approach is emerging if you recall the distinction I offered early on in *Chopstick*.

The signs show fissures emerging in the network TV advertising business. Smaller network television audiences and less advertising opportunities are driving *increased* pricing for traditional advertising. This is like the newspaper industry cutting the number of papers printed by say 10 percent, and then raising the cost to buy papers based on the reduced number of papers available to purchase. False logic is at work here, which ignores new social media, new ways of reaching people. And most important, new ways of going beyond the "80" we discussed before, reaching the "20," and doing it profitably.

So what is the outlook here? In the network TV advertising business, reaching the long tail and doing it effectively demands a new approach, "outside the room" thinking, driven by more precise analytics and performance metrics. New services, such as those offered by Google TV, Microsoft's Navic Networks, and SpotRunner, are emerging, and these are names not traditionally mentioned in the network TV advertising sector. They are reshaping the advertising business and will help define the evolving future business models.

Again we see the solutions emerging from *entrepreneurial* rather than *traditional* firms, who are comfortable doing business as usual and typically slower to embrace next-generation technology and "thinking." This is not true for all players and all sectors, but does apply more often than not.

Building Entrepreneurial Age Relationships with Customers

Today's entrepreneurial age demands that marketers employ social media based marketing tools, forging new relationships with customers that go well beyond what is done today.

Rick Edelman is founder and CEO of Edelman PR, a highly successful PR firm headquartered in the Washington, D.C., metropolitan area. In a speech when accepting the National Public Relations Achievement Award in April 2006, it was reported that Edelman, a prolific blogger and social media driver, takes exception to the traditional perception of the PR "spin doctor," emphasizing that PR must employ a "peer pressure" driven relationship between companies and their customers. Simply put, smart PR firms must embrace the concept of using social media and peer pressure to link and engage customers with their peers and those they trust—company employees, advocates, third parties, "New Influencers," and others. To back this up, Edelman reported the results of his Trust Barometer Survey, which showed "... *in the U.S. a "person like yourself" <peer> was trusted by 22 percent of the respondents as recently as 2003, while in this year's study, 68 percent said they trusted a peer.*"[23]

Creating new ways to communicate with your customers and prospects, developing *peer level*, trusted relationships is really what the social media is all about. A powerful tool that should be embraced by all organizations, both large and small.

The Pervasiveness of Social Media

As mentioned before, I find the pervasiveness and reach of the new social media, particularly blogs, are really not well understood by many. Some still believe these are a fad, a helpful tool to *complement* traditional ways of marketing, advertising, and supporting customers. There are enough war stories out there—companies like Dell, AOL, and others that bloggers have pursued forcing these companies and others to quickly muster resources and develop strategies to respond. Yesterday, handling public relations issues meant issuing press releases, holding press conferences, conducting interviews with TV pundits, and so on. Not so easy today given the global expansiveness and reach of social media and blogs. Just look at some numbers here.

Neilsen is in the ratings business, and their BuzzMetrics service tracks blog posts and links to other blogs. How blogs interconnect, what posts appear on multiple blogs provides powerful insights that often go beyond the information actually posted. The bottom line—Nielsen's service, one of many offered, helps companies understand what is being said about their products and other issues relevant to their business.

Look at the complexity here. The Nielsen service monitors thirty million blogs worldwide yielding five hundred thousand to one million daily posts, and analyzes the results to provide action-able data to clients.[24] Amazing when you look at the scale here. But we are only at the starting point here in the long tail marketing revolution. Most of today's analytics use what is called deductive analysis. Simply put, you define certain rules to identify or cata-log buyers—maybe by income, geographic area, type of products they buy or own, sites they visit, and so on. These "rules" are used to filter the total population of users to identify potential targets. Very large scale here and many assumptions are needed, but the deductive approach is well proven and a *traditional*, widely used technique.

In 2008, I led a company offering powerful predictive analytics (PA) capabilities. Predictive analytics starts with basic rules and analyzes the data to develop *new* rules based on the actual data and outcomes. PA tools analyze data relationships to *drive the creation of new rules*, which can then be applied going forward. So if a company has a product that is missing sales targets, you can use PA to analyze who *actually* bought the product, identify the buyers' profile and purchase decision factors, and identify buying decision data that you were *not* aware of up front. These new rules drive creation of *new* strategies to reach *new* customers. In the health care sector, for example, you can use PA techniques to identify what medications work best for what patients, and what medica-tions specific patients should avoid, again based on decision data you were *not* aware of up front. In the health care sector, PA tools have significant potential to improve costly new drug clinical trial processes, help identify adverse drug interactions, and provide the foundation for a number of new, exciting, personalized "long tail" medication initiatives.

While these are exciting capabilities, couple these analytics with social media, and the wealth of marketing data now possible promises to reshape how customers' needs are addressed in all sectors. I foresee smaller, nimble, agile entrepreneurial firms play-ing a more significant role here, particularly in several high-growth sectors including financial services, energy, and health care.

Reaching new markets, serving individual customer needs, cre-ating profitable niche business opportunities—these are happen-ing now, and these trends will accelerate driven by the long tail marketing and social media revolutions.

oℕo

Chapter 8

Strategic Plans and Not-So-Strategic Plans

The greatest danger for most of us is not that our aim is too high
and we miss it, but that it is too low and we achieve it.
Michelangelo

Is Strategy Planning an Anachronism?

Strategic planning sounds like an anachronism. Talking about a strategic plan in today's high-speed, technology-driven, entre-preneurial-fueled world sounds like we are going backward. After all, with tsunami-like, ground-changing events happening quickly on every front—markets, technology, competition, regulatory— any strategic plan would be obsolete before the ink barely dries. Or so you would think. And if so, why bother?

Well, achieving success long term means understanding what's really happening in the industry and what is needed to win. Easy words to say—much harder to do. We often we go for achieving an immediate short-term target, at the expense of long-term profit, strategic position, customer satisfaction, and sometimes company survival. This is particularly true for entrepreneurial firms where making the "first million" may be the goal.

But remember more than half of all new ventures fail within three years. You can trace many of these failures to misunderstand-ing the market opportunity, competitive environment, and choos-ing incorrect long-term strategies needed to survive and prosper. That is the focus of the strategic-planning process and why it is essential.

You may recall what I said in the preface of *Chopstick,* and this is a point I will reinforce again: there are no magic bullets for success, no rule that guarantees success and works in all cases. It would be great if there was, but there is not. The only rule is there are no simple rules. You learn, no matter what your level of seniority and experience, by sharing perspectives on best prac-tices, rather than using firm rules. Management science is in some ways a misnomer—science implies a mathematical rigor, repeat-ability. That is often not reality in the business world.

If you think I am going too far on this point, let's look at what many believe is a simple strategy-planning "rule" for success. Repeated so often this is now urban legend as a winning strategy for companies. It goes something like this:

> *Leading firms listen to their customers. Securing customer feedback helps firms understand customers' needs, today and future, identify issues and new opportunities. Valuable input here that firms should use to drive their strategy, business, and technology plans and maximize value creation.*

Sounds good. But suppose after listening to your customers, you aggressively invest in new technologies that customers want, you invest in those innovation areas that promised the best returns, you meet customer expectations. You have done it all right and minimized risk. But look at others that have also done it right, solidly managed firms such as Xerox, Sears, and Digital Equipment Corp (DEC), among others. Research suggests the fact these companies had good management, listened to their customers, and did the right things, and that was the reason they failed to see the train wreck coming in their respective businesses and lost their leadership position. Sounds counterintuitive and it is. The fact is these and many other well-managed, leading companies failed to understand the principles of disruptive innovation, defining how technology will go beyond just changing your business, but radically reshape markets creating both opportunities and challenges for your current business.

Strategic Planning Process vs. Strategic Plan

I see an important distinction here that will become clear. My experience echoes the philosophy of General Dwight D. Eisenhower when preparing for D-Day. Obviously an amazing planning effort—thousands of soldiers and armament, multiple countries and cultures, a sea to cross, weather uncertainties, where to land, and examine hundreds of "what-ifs." When the final plan was drawn up, General Eisenhower remarked, "The plan is nothing; the planning process is everything."

Unfortunately, these words are lost on many, particularly among entrepreneurial firms. The strategic planning process is fundamental to understand the changing entrepreneurial age market drivers and respond forcefully. You recall my discussion with the Jupiter management team (chapter 2). While at a high level here, my objective was really to move beyond the plan and into the process of fleshing out the underlying drivers, issues, and opportunities before setting a firm direction. While high level, this is a good example of what I mean by the strategy-planning process. Very important message here.

The Eight Key Questions

Think about your current business, or perhaps a new venture you feel is the "next Google," and see if you and your team have answers to the following questions:

1. What is our corporate mission—what do we "want to be"?
2. What is market size and segmentation for our business?
3. What are the long-term growth, pricing, revenue, and market share projections?
4. Who are our competitors? What is their respective share, and who are major threats?
5. What is our business model, and how do we create earnings and value?
6. What are our strategies?
7. How do we use technology—what changes are needed?
8. What is our financial plan? How much goes in; when does it go in; how much goes out; when does it come out? (That is my entrepreneurial age shorthand to summarize the entire financial planning process.)

Look closely at the above eight questions, and you realize you are looking at a "rough" business plan outline. Maybe missing some sections such as management team, organization structure, offices, and so on. But a close look shows we really do capture the key business plan drivers here. And my experience with many early-stage firms such as the Jupiter team discussed in chapter 2 is they would embrace the above as the business plan and, when completed, take the entire staff out to lunch, be glad to put the planning process behind them, and get busy doing "real" work creating the next Google.

Many Fortune 1000 firms have followed the same thinking. Putting their traditional businesses on "cruise control," thinking what they do today and how they do it will not change—maybe grow faster, maybe slower, maybe offer some new features wanted by customers, maybe branch out to other sectors. But really the same core business—let's not do anything to rock the boat or change too much here. Change is tough, risky, and can hurt us. Unfortunately, this is seductive and dangerous thinking in today's entrepreneurial age for all firms, both large and small.

I agree the above eight questions do really outline a business plan, and the same thinking for many really does provide the basis for the company's strategic plan. I also understand that you may have bound your plan in a attractive printed binder to reinforce commitment to "the plan," distributed copies to the management team, and announced its creation with some flourish—I have done this many times myself. Done properly, the company's strategic plan and a clearly defined, motivating vision really helps drive a company's success, provides the company's perspective on where it is headed, what it considers important, what is the company culture, what businesses it is in today, and what future business will be pursued. Again, if done properly, business plans will dovetail directly with the company's overall strategic plan. That is the good news.

The "Incomplete" Planning Process

The bad news is your planning process here is incomplete. To assume otherwise is dangerous thinking given industry changes we see, failure rates on new business ventures, and how today's changes are gouging and dismembering major firms that should have known better (think about pre-bailout General Motors here).

So after you go through your white board sessions fleshing out answers to these eight questions, I suggest hold off a bit on the "planning is all behind us" luncheon with your team, and think about some other perspectives I want to share with you in this chapter.

The "Not So Strategic Plan"

The above planning process really defines what I call the *not so strategic plan*. To win, you need to develop a strategic plan. We still have a ways to go here. I have found among many emerging companies and students this term sticks and expect it may with you also. Surprisingly, many larger firms also believe their strategic planning process is complete and optimized. So exactly what is missing here? How do we enhance our plan to create a strategic plan that optimizes positioning given today's entrepreneurial age groundswell changes?

Going back to your *not so strategic plan*, you really need to address two more factors. And this is true for both entrepreneurial ventures as well as major firms. First, you need to understand, and I mean really understand, the competitive environment. Not just who are the competitors, how large they are, and who has what market share as many business plans do. Competitive forces define profitability and long-time business potential, really the "guts" of any business opportunity. Very high exposure area here and you want to understand how this is done, what tools are used, and what you need to know. We will review this in chapter 11 when we discuss Porter's Five Forces Model and other tools.

The second factor that you need to address is the issue of disruptive innovation. In some sectors, disruptive innovation *is* the "eight hundred pound gorilla in the room." You ignore it at your own peril. Imagine you are a member of the Redbox management team, and you are brainstorming to develop next year's strategic plan. Redbox, as most know, offers low cost (one dollar a night) DVD rentals using DVD vending machines located in supermarkets and other retail sites. They have several "eight hundred pound, disruptive innovation gorillas in the room," such as video on demand offered by cable companies, Internet TV offerings, free downloadable movies, and bundled video on demand with telephone services. Each of these is a disruptive innovation that impacts the Redbox current business model and must be addressed. It appears they may be facing a *herd* of gorillas.

Disruptive Innovation: A Pharmaceutical Sector Perspective

The above is a relatively simple example of disruptive innovation primarily focusing on alternative business models. Often however, understanding, with precision, how your business will change is much more complex and cannot be precisely defined. Look at the pharmaceutical industry, for example, which includes two primary sectors—therapeutics (i.e., drugs) and diagnostics.

Therapeutics is the pharmaceutical firms' traditional business, reported to be about a $400 to $450 billion market. Compare that to the diagnostics business, which includes several hundred companies, including many early stage entrepreneurial companies. Revenue estimates vary, but total diagnostic sector revenues today are estimated at less than $30 billion, or less than 10 percent of a major pharmas traditional business. But diagnostics reduces health care costs, and many exciting developments are emerging providing the tools needed to improve early disease detection.

For example, we now see new biomarker technology, showing genetic "signatures," is now moving us closer to personalized medicine. What that means is upfront diagnostics will reap significant benefits for people, improve health care quality, and reduce overall costs for all including pharmaceutical firms. While this all sounds good, for a pharmaceutical company, this is disruptive innovation, changes that threaten the company's *traditional* revenue base. So how should a pharmaceutical firm respond to these market shifts? Should they aggressively pursue new diagnostic market opportunities to minimize impact on their core business? Should they reposition their business to adapt to the new opportunities? Remember, much of the diagnostics market growth, particularly in the personalized medicine areas, has been driven by smaller, more agile, entrepreneurial firms who really have an inside track for the moment, positioning to play a key long-term role in the rapidly growing diagnostics market segment.

I often describe disruptive innovation as a freight train. Understanding what freight trains are coming down the same track, how you can avoid a smash-up and, in some cases, hitch a ride are the key points to keep in mind here.

Strategic Vision Drives a Strategic Plan

So what exactly what is a strategic vision, why do we need it, how do we get it, can we ever lose it, and how do we use it? This is another one of those topics that could be another book, and if you doubt that, go into any mega-bookstore, look at the nonfiction best sellers, and count the number of new books with the words *strategy* or *vision* in the title—they line the bookshelves. Pump in strategic vision in Amazon's search engine and you will get more than six hundred titles, and I am sure many more are in the pipeline

Look at seemingly well-positioned new ventures and ask yourself the following question: Assuming the companies are in the right industry, at the right time, why does one company enjoy explosive success and another failure? We discussed some reasons earlier in *Chopstick* mostly focusing on strategy, innovation, and managing change. Even when you do all the right things, have the right team with what many believe is an excellent plan, business sometimes fails. Often inadequate financial resources are blamed with words like "… our business was on target, our business model met expectations, we were attracting customers, but we just ran out of funding." Sort of like the doctor saying the operation went well but the patient died.

Let's back up here. Assuming at the outset the cash financing met my venture-funding litmus test, i.e., divide revenue forecasts by two, multiply expense forecasts by two, and shift all milestones one year to the right—if your business model still holds up, you should have sufficient funding. The odds are you will make it assuming your plan has any merit at all and you have an experienced management team.

So go back to my initial questions here: What separates winners from the losers? Why do some companies go down in flames, performing poorly in strong markets?

Winners vs. Losers

Creating and sustaining a vision plays a key role. Sure, we can create a vision, often driven by a senior officer's sheer personality in many emerging companies. But the challenges are twofold. First, ensuring management buy-in, getting the troops pointed in the same direction. Mountains can be moved by an organization that is "in tune," resonant with its creative visionary. Even better when the creative visionary is, in fact, in charge of the organization, and sometimes this is not the case.

Second, and just as important, is what I call defensibility of vision. Why is the vision correct; what is the justification; can it be dissected, put back together, and stand the test of reasonableness to validate assumptions, projections, and outlook? Tough questions but answer them correctly and things happen. You get credibility with your team, and organizational resonance takes over. You get credibility with investors, so if plans change, and we all know they do, you can go back to the well and keep your head up high, even while walking in with hat in hand.

Unfortunately, many organizations are founded on an idea, a business concept, not fleshed out in any real detail. And this idea is presented as the vision for the business. Ideas are not opportunities as we have seen, and this confusion is often costly. Usually this vision starts out with words like "... I foresee a great market opportunity to sell new low-end PCs for the home consumer market."

Depending on who says this, this may end up being the strategic vision for the business, and I have been involved in some of these. No vetting, no real analysis, just gut feel, or "fingerspitzengefuhl" by a charismatic founder. Now let's look at someone who knows how to get this right—Steve Jobs.

The Steve Jobs Attribute: Articulating The Vision

Steve Jobs is a great model showing how a leader articulates a vision that's interesting, dynamic, and compelling. Staying the course, keeping troops rallied when the going gets rough, and motivating people to stay—these are the "Steve Jobs Attribute," a term coined by Ben Horowitz of VC firm Andreessen Horowitz.[25] Look at what Jobs has accomplished. He kept employees at NeXT while the business was crumbling, and he kept the Apple staff engaged to stay with him while the company was weeks away from bankruptcy. An outstanding example of successfully developing and executing a strategic vision.[26]

Chapter 9

Precision Thinking: Understanding Set, Drift, Errors in "Business" Navigation—Are We Heading for the Bahamas or Portugal?

You can do everything right, strictly according to procedure, on the ocean, and it'll still kill you, but if you are a good navigator, at least you'll know where you were when you died.
Justin Scott
The Shipkiller

Clarity, Consistency, Precision, and Fuzzy Thinking

Clarity, consistency, and precision drive effective business decisions, and that is particularly true for securing new venture funding. By contrast, what I call "fuzzy thinking" is an impediment that works against you and holds you back. And what exactly is fuzzy thinking? Let me share some perspectives that I think will make this clear.

Case study analysis is a powerful learning tool used when teaching advanced business strategy and entrepreneurship courses. Typically, classes are organized into teams consisting of four or five students. Each team develops an analysis and presentation reviewing the team's findings and recommendations. I often use Harvard Business School case studies addressing business topics such as Google's corporate mission and growth strategies; GE Medical Systems' China market entry strategy; Pandesic, a new venture launched by SAP and Intel; and many other case studies also from Harvard Business School and other institutions.[27] This is an excellent teaching tool that I am now using to develop a new global entrepreneurial management seminar program, building on many of the concepts discussed in *Chopstick*.

Typically each team is given fifteen minutes to present their case study analysis; they are timed with a "hard stop." They must summarize the case, identify the issues, assess the current strategies and results, and recommend and defend new strategies as appropriate. I position each team as a management consulting firm conducting a business review for the company's board of directors. Often I invite senior colleagues to critique and provide their feedback on the presentations. I caution all teams to avoid fuzzy thinking and emphasize "clarity, consistency, and precision" when making these presentations. I may sound rigid and over the top here, but my experience is fuzzy thinking is a killer of many business presentations and careers as well. This is a great learning experience. Forcing a tight time limit helps drive precision thinking.

You would expect with all my reinforcement here, fuzzy thinking would not be a problem—at least not in these brief and hopefully tight presentations. Not so. I have developed a running list of language that sends a loud and clear fuzzy thinking signal and should be avoided, and I share this with students at the start of each semester. Here is a sample of what I mean—these comments are taken from actual case study presentations:

- *"... company has very high debt"*

How high is high? What does this mean? Better to show amount and best to also show trends. Maybe say, "...company has $10 billion debt, up from $8 billion a year ago."

- *"Based on our analysis, it is obvious that the problem (or solution) is ..."*

Saying something is "obvious" sends a fuzzy thinking signal that something is missing here. This is a good habit to lose if you have this affliction. Maybe your finding is obvious to you, but this language sends a signal to management that you do not have clear understanding of the basic drivers and what is happening. You need more clarity; avoid the "obvious" word at all cost unless you can strongly defend and quantify.

- *"... we recommend company pursue a functional level strategy to capitalize on the company's competitive edge (also called 'distinctive competency')"*

Maybe a good idea or maybe not—no one can really tell hearing this. What functional strategy, e.g., marketing, R&D, production, and so on, should the company build upon with your recommended plan. And exactly what do you recommend they do?

You need to be more precise here. It would be better to say something like "... company should pursue functional level strategy emphasizing expanded product sales support building on their extensive sales network..."

- *"... government segment generates higher margin than consumer segment"*

How much more? Is it significant? Why should we care?

- *"... growing faster than previous years"*

Same comments as above.

- *"... important to focus on both markets"*

Why? It may be important to you but not necessarily to those listening to you unless you defend this assertion.

Some Helpful Presentation Tips to Improve Clarity and Precision

And here are some general tips that I usually share to tighten these case study presentations to improve clarity, consistency, and precision:

- *Tighten and refine the logic of the business case you are building and ensure this "maps" to your presentation*

For example, suppose you initially identify profit expansion as the most critical need. Keep that focus throughout—show how what you are proposing will expand profits. Avoid changing to recommend, for example, that revenue growth is the key strategy driver—use consistent metrics and recommended strategies to reinforce your assertions and avoid the fuzzy thinking problem. This is an easy mistake to make.

- *Keep your focus solely on the <u>most</u> important, defensible directions and recommended strategies to address the company's needs*

You should maintain a laserlike focus on the most critical, substantive issues. Say business profitability is a key concern—you need to review the issue and provide your recommendations. While you may have ideas on how human resources should also be restructured to develop a future labor pool, hold the temptation to divert and stay on course. You have a tight time window; focusing on the most critical issues is essential to build strong, clearly defined business proposals.

- *Keep your focus solely on "selling" your recommended, defensible directions and strategies*

Remember other options *always* exist and can be chosen rather than what you are proposing. And there is almost always a "do nothing" strategy, described with words like: "… maybe we should make no investment at this time and study this further" or "… we seem to have no agreement on your analysis and recommendations—let's table this for now." Your job is to maintain a laserlike focus on your recommended directions and secure buy-in for your plan. Do not say there are other recommended strategy options unless you are prepared to defend, in detail, why you have not selected these other options.

What you are showing is, by your definition, the optimum strategy. Always keep in mind you only impact your own argument if you overemphasize other options.

- *Creating logical, defensible recommendations is essential, but effectively communicating your recommendations is just as important*

It is good discipline to *always* assume you have limited time— your colleagues will also appreciate this. Suppose you propose three key strategies. You should first review all three in a high-level bullet format, presenting highlights of each. After you do this, and only after you summarize each, you then focus on the first strategy, add three to four subbullets, and explain each.

So why go through this disciplined effort; why not just review each strategy in detail, move to the next, and summarize? It sounds like a more direct approach and that it is.

But your presentation is not measured on directness, but rather whether you secure buy-in on your analysis and recommendations. My recommended approach typically helps avoid two traps. First, suppose you review the first strategy in detail, and your assumptions and recommendations are questioned. You may respond with something like "... your concerns are answered when we get to discussing our third strategy, so hold your question for now." Not a good position to be in, particularly if it happens several times as you proceed.

Second, if you review your first strategy in detail, you may generate strong discussion—both positive and negative—which may take over your presentation, and you run out of time. Always preferable to present the whole story as you want it to be positioned and "stay on message."

One effective approach I recommend is a "peel the onion" presentation strategy. What I mean here follows for a sample case study.

"Peel the Onion" Presentation Strategy for Communicating Strategies

Suppose you are asked to develop recommended strategies for the Grassroots Lawnmower Company to improve profitability. Grassroots is a fictitious company I use to illustrate strategy management tools and concepts. The team's recommended presentation may go something like this:

"We propose three improvement strategies. The first strategy proposes to develop the Grassroots Galaxy, a new flagship, high-end lawnmower product, which builds upon Grassroots' competitive edge (i.e., distinctive competencies) in R&D and manufacturing. The second strategy proposes to fill in the Grassroots product line at the low end, proposing a new Grassroots Starcraft mass-market model and pursuing a cost leadership strategy in two U.S. regional markets. Our third strategy emphasizes the need to further increase our R&D capabilities related to computers, electronic sensors, and next gen technologies, and we will pursue a joint R&D agreement with two target technology companies. Our strategy plan will enable us, within twenty-four months, to achieve market share of 44 percent, up from 35 percent today, and increase net income by about 18 percent to $19 million." (This is the highest level of strategy review.)

Next, go back and review the first strategy, creating the new high-end product—describe R&D to create the new product, review features and competitive analysis, review issues and opportunities. Repeat for other strategies. (This is the next level.)

Provide any more detail that supports your case and why your strategy selection is best. (This is the final level.)

What you are doing here is "peeling the onion"—describing the summary, drilling down the next level, and so on using a disciplined structure. An effective tool to present complex projects and secure buy-in within a short time window.

Clarity, consistency, and effective communications—the above are relatively simple tools and techniques used to achieve a level of precision that I believe are critically important entrepreneurial management skills. And this applies both for business school graduates, as well as seasoned new venture business professionals at all levels.

The Cover All Bases (CAB) Principle

You need precision when building and communicating your business proposals, be they case studies, new venture business plans, or maybe a large-scale project for which you are seeking approval.

I have found the Cover All Bases (CAB) Principle a helpful tool to avoid the fuzzy thinking trap. For example, suppose you want to get support for new technology venture in your company. You make the point that the market for the new technology market is large and growing quickly. Your company has patents and resources to succeed, and you have the management team in place. It sounds impressive, but it's not good enough yet.

My caution is to remember the CAB Principle here. Tell me who the competition is, how will they respond, what happens to your core business if you pursue this, what are the opportunity costs here, what is the long-term outlook—I can keep going here and so can those you are presenting to. Presenting new business ideas without addressing these and other basic questions shows fuzzy thinking, and violates the CAB Principle—the need to thoroughly cover all details, be ready to go in back-up mode, and give them no place to go.

To further reinforce the need for precision thinking, I often compare the challenges of developing a new business direction similar in many ways to navigating a boat. As a longtime boater, I find nautical analogies helpful to explain business rules and techniques.

Charting a Course to the Bahamas, Not Portugal

Developing business plans that plot a course, just as in navigation, demand precision, understanding of how external factors—such as market forces, competition, technology, regulation, and other drivers—impact the "course." You may have a great product strategy, but competition and other external market forces will impact long-term business success. You must understand and define their impact.

Suppose you want to chart a course from Palm Beach, Florida, to the Bahamas. You establish a heading, which can be easily determined using a navigational chart and looking at the compass "rose." Maybe you proceed on a heading of 120 degrees, or in a southeast direction—90 degrees is east and 180 degrees is heading south. You probably look forward to arriving before dinner, maybe having a piña colada while hanging out at Goombay Mama's, the casino lounge at the Marriot's Resort and Crystal Palace Casino. Well, if you really want to get there, hopefully you also looked at two other navigational forces—"set" and "drift"—external factors that may affect your journey.

"Drift" is the speed of the current usually expressed in knots (roughly equal to miles per hour). "Set" is the direction or heading in degrees of the currents you encounter during your journey. If drift is high and the set or direction of the current is not in the same direction you are going, your course is changed. And sometimes these changes are significant. When charting a course, drift and set are calculated, and a ship's course is adjusted to compensate. Fuzzy thinking doesn't work well on the water or in business.

So for your planned journey to the Bahamas, if you proceed on the planned 120-degree southeast heading and the direction or "set" of the current is northerly, you may miss the Bahamas and maybe catch a northerly small island. If the speed or "drift" of the current is also fast, you will most likely miss the Bahamas entirely. Look at a map of the Caribbean and Atlantic Ocean and this will be clear. You are heading for open waters and the European continent.

So if you really plan on pursuing a course from Palm Beach to the Bahamas and you ignore the external factors of set and drift, you will probably end up in Portugal, not the Bahamas, maybe sipping a glass of Vinho Verde, Portugal's well-known green wine and, if you are fortunate, perhaps sitting at the bar of the luxurious five-star Martinhai Beach Resort and Hotel in the historic seaside town of Sagres. Really nice place to go, just not where you were planning to be. In this case, you missed your mark by ignoring critical external factors. Same with business planning—fuzzy thinking has no place in today's business environment.

So if you plan on building a business case for a new venture proposing to build a network device capturing Internet-based TV from anywhere on the planet, or a next-generation chicken broiler, you had better understand external factors like technology shifts, competitive alternatives, including TV sets with integrated Internet links or other ways of cooking chickens—I think you get the point here. These factors impact the "business navigation" course you have carefully planned. You need to drill down and understand where these factors will take you and what you need to do to stay on course. Fuzzy thinking has no place in the new venture planning process if you want to win.

Clarity, consistency, and precision thinking are the critical skills needed to survive and prosper in today's morphing marketplace. The bottom line here—make sure you develop your precision thinking skills if you want to improve your success rate in business. Portugal is a real nice place to visit, particularly in the springtime, but not when your destination is the Bahamas.

❧

Chapter 10

Competition: Knowing When to Circle the Wagons and Which Wagons to Circle

The ability to learn faster than your competitors may be the only sustainable competitive advantage.
Arie de Geus[28]

A Competitive Analysis Primer

Competition is tough. To think otherwise is an easy trap to fall into. Look at competition from various perspectives, and I think you will see my point.

One challenge is understanding exactly who the competition is. Often not so easy these days with markets morphing, explosive technology changes, and powerful global competitors. I often reinforce this point recalling an analogy I first heard years ago in a marketing conference. The speaker told the story of two hunters being chased into the tent by the raging bear. About to be eaten, one hunter reaches for his gun; the other hunter reaches for his sneakers. Saying that he cannot outrun the bear, the hunter asks his companion why he was putting on his sneakers and not getting his gun. The other hunter says, "I don't have to run faster than the bear; I just have to run faster than you." He clearly knows his competition in this battle. When attacked by competition, you also better know who your competitors are, when to put on your sneakers and run, and when to hold your ground and shoot. Easy words to say, often much harder to do today.

Historically, this was a more manageable process with traditional stable markets, an identifiable mix of small to mega competitors, and a forecastable technology outlook. Some market surprises, new entrants, and market shifts maybe, but for the most part, in most sectors traditional competitive and market analysis worked well for decades. Having spent many years managing lines of business within the information industry, competitive analysis and market planning were often developed by lower-level marketing staff and submitted to senior staff for review and approval. Add a growth rate to last year's numbers and you generated next year's numbers. Spreadsheet formulas, not detailed market or competitive analysis, met the planning needs here.

The *traditional* competitive analysis thought process had many variations but for most companies went something like this:

- What is the market size for my product (the addressable market)?
- What is the segment of the total market my company targets (the addressed market)?
- What other competitors are addressing my market segment?
- What portion of the market does my company capture vis-à-vis competitors (market share)?
- How has my market share varied during the one-year, three-year, and five-year periods?
- If we are *increasing* market share, do we need to take any actions to maintain and grow market share?
- If we are *decreasing* market share, what actions do we need to take to retain market share and offset competition?
- How do our product features compare to competition? Are we leaders or laggards?
- What are the pricing and profitability metrics? Are we maintaining market share by cutting prices and reducing earnings or adding more features; are competitors increasing market share by cutting prices or adding more features; is market size increasing enabling our earning goals to be met with reduced market share?

The above is a simplified analysis showing how traditional competitive analysis was performed. Other planning tools and analytics support these planning efforts, but for the most part, in many stable market sectors, the above captures the essence of the traditional process. And this process applied to early stage ventures, as well as lines of business within major corporations. If a long track record of established sales exists for a product, the thinking was why bother doing more analysis and going much further than the above.

No more. That was yesterday. While these traditional tools are still used and helpful, there are not one but a number of "eight hundred pound gorillas" in the room that must also be addressed. Let's discuss a few.

Three "Eight Hundred Pound Gorillas" in the Room

First, today all markets are evolving. It's not good enough to assume your market is stable and always will be. Understanding competition demands understanding the environment within which companies operate. Is this a growing market? Is there "intense" competition that will drive down profits? What is the threat of new entrants? What is the threat of substitute products? We will revisit these questions in chapter 11. Properly used, the Five Forces Analysis Model is a powerful tool to address one "eight hundred pound gorilla" in the room—we may be doing well today, but what is the competitive environment outlook, what is *really* happening out there, and is this an attractive profitable market?

Moving on to a second "eight hundred pound gorilla"— suppose your company has done well in the past, future market shares are encouraging, and the competitive environment looks attractive; how are you *really* positioned, what are the opportunities and threats you should expect ahead, and what are your strengths and weaknesses? As we will see shortly in chapter 11, these questions provide the foundation for a SWOT analysis (i.e., analysis of a company's strengths, weaknesses, opportunities, and threats) to further tighten and link competitive analysis and strategy development. Keep in mind I am simplifying this process for discussion purposes. I have been involved in SWOT analyses involving multiple products and channels, examining a wide range of what-ifs, looking at strategy and earnings impact, complex alternative pricing models, and so on. This really is a powerful, useful analysis tool.

Finally, a third and most important "eight hundred pound gorilla" is technology innovation. You recall our discussion in chapter 5 about the need to understand where you are on the innovation staircase. Have you left the first entry-level step and are you heading up the growth staircase? Is there room for further market growth? How close are you to reaching the next level, market maturity?

Most important, are there any *entirely new staircases* emerging out there that may impact you? And if so, what are your strategy options? Remember our discussion about Blockbuster in chapter 7. Refining their business model, developing new ways to compete in the video rental market, they performed well, going up their sector's "innovation staircase." But then they crashed, facing an innovative, Internet-based competitor, Netflix, changing the rules of the game. New staircase, new rules and the need to adapt to survive.

To also reinforce this point, remember NCR discussed in chapter 5 who viewed the emergence of computer technology as "enhancing" their electromechanical cash register (ECR) business, helping them accelerate up the innovation staircase. Wrong decision—computer technology created a *new* innovation staircase that subsumed both NCR and the ECR market. Understanding what other innovation staircases are out there that may either impact your business or create new ones is critical and, in my experience, often not properly addressed.

Keep in mind the objective of these analyses is not to get firm yes or no answers, but rather to understand, using an organized approach, the key drivers shaping your product's competitive landscape. Ensuring the entire management team is fully engaged during this process is the approach used by leading firms and makes sense. Remember the words of General and Former President Dwight D. Eisenhower during the D-Day planning effort mentioned earlier: *"The planning process is everything; the plan is nothing."*

Obviously he exaggerated a bit, the D-Day invasion plan was critically important, but the former president does make the key point that working through a structured planning process, engaging the management team and staff to contribute is invaluable to assess the competitive landscape, understand where the "landmines" are, and develop winning strategies.

While a comprehensive discussion of competitive analysis is beyond the scope of this book given space limitations, understanding traditional market and competitive analysis tools coupled with how Porter's Five Forces Analysis Model and SWOT analysis complement the process is a good starting point. We will discuss these in the next chapter.

Competitive Analysis for Emerging Firms: Is This Really Necessary?

Simple answer here: yes. I understand the argument that emerging firms are not Coca-Cola and do not have the planning resources or business scale to justify these efforts. Working with many new ventures and investors, it is clear to me, however, that dissecting markets and competition, going well beyond traditional market share-driven planning efforts, using the above and other planning tools to more precisely define your business sends a powerful message to investors and stakeholders. That is the standard I have used for years with all ventures I am involved with, and it does work. Compare this to the following typical competitive analysis scenario we often see with early stage firms:

> *Our market analysis shows a potential market of 1,000,000 users who, based on focus groups, will pay $10 for our product. We have two competitors who offer fewer features, and we conservatively estimate we can capture 2 percent of the market increasing to 5 percent by year 3. Year 1 revenues are projected at $200,000 (2 percent x 1,000,000 users x $10 per product sale) increasing to $500,000 by year 2.*

The above analysis falls short in many ways and is not defensible without more work, using the planning tools described above and addressing the "eight hundred pound gorillas in the room." Unfortunately, my experience suggests emerging firms often fail here, and educating emerging company management on how market leaders address these challenges provides real benefits to help grow emerging firms both in the United States and developing countries. We will discuss this further in chapter 11.

These techniques can typically be learned in an advanced business strategy undergraduate or graduate course at most leading business schools. Teaching these courses at several universities since 2002, using Harvard Business School and other case studies, I have observed that understanding these analysis tools, the "laws of business" as described earlier, improves management skills and clearly provides an "edge."

Avoiding the "Paralysis by Analysis" Problem

If you know a dog has fleas, the first thing you do is take action to treat the fleas—don't start a procedure to determine the cause of the fleas. Action is emphasized in today's unpredictable, high-energy environment; you need to address immediate, obvious problems before they "kill the dog."

You have to make decisions, often with incomplete data. Middle of the road inaction really doesn't work in today's global entrepreneurial markets. Or as so eloquently said by the former head of the Texas Agriculture Commission Jim Hightower, "...Ain't nothing in the middle of the road but yellow stripes and dead armadillos."

What the above suggests is you do have to be careful by not carrying planning too far. While I see this often in major firms with a large number of planning and analysis staff, it is most troublesome in emerging firms with limited resources. Often you cannot delay in responding to market challenges and opportunities, and time is of the essence. "Paralysis by analysis" creates failure as market opportunities are missed, new competition emerges, and market share erodes.

Sometimes you may not get the decision exactly right and on target or break any records, but like the cross-eyed javelin thrower, at least by taking action you will get attention. As most of us know, with battle scars to prove it, to ensure survival in today's dynamic global entrepreneurial age, it is better to "beg forgiveness rather than ask permission" when responding to market needs and competition.

Properly managed, emerging firms really do have a nimbleness that is not easily matched by major competitors, who assess new competitive developments through the prism of how these changes impact their existing lines of business and processes.

∽✺∾

Chapter 11

Laws of Management Strategy: Not Repealed for New Business Ventures—Porters Five Forces Model and Other Tools

Perception is strong and sight weak. In strategy it is
important to see distant things as if they were close
and to take a distanced view of close things.
Miyamoto Musashi (1584–1645)
Legendary Japanese swordsman

The "Seductiveness" of New Ventures

Whether we have two talented engineers in a garage developing the next Internet-based social network or a group of friends conceiving a new device linking to the Internet, the business development process is pretty much the same. Let's go back to the Jupiter Model 2.0 device discussed in chapter 2 that links to the Internet and can download videos from anywhere on the planet. Assume you were a member of the management team, a highly energized entrepreneurial team, and the objective was to now define the scale of opportunity here.

Suppose your analysis of market statistics shows a potential of ten million households may buy the new device. Your team estimates the device will sell for $100 with a $10 per month subscription fee. You feel this is conservative since you are assuming after one year, Jupiter will capture only 1 percent of the market. That means you will have installed one hundred thousand units (1 percent of ten million households). At a price $100 each, you will have created $10 million in product sales and a recurring revenue base of $1 million per month (one hundred thousand units each paying $10 per month); this is a potential $12 million annual recurring revenue business.

Assuming you earn 10 percent profit after tax, your business looks attractive. And you only captured 1 percent of the market here; surely this is conservative, and your team feels you may even do better here. You estimate you need $1.2 million to launch the business, and you prepare the business plan. If you are fortunate may attract angel funding from friends and family or FF (sometimes called FFF or "Friends, Family, and Fools"—harsher perhaps, but for some ventures often more accurate).

I have worked with many ventures in diverse market sectors, and most follow similar patterns. Often a seductive process as emphasized before. The challenge is to get past the technology "gee-whiz" factors, keep the entrepreneurial enthusiasm "firing on all cylinders," but also use more traditional management processes to accurately assess the opportunity and develop a successful execution plan. Moving entrepreneurial staff to employ more traditional management thinking is often easier to say than do.

Traditional Management "Laws" Are Not Repealed

We may like to think so, but the traditional laws of management are *not* repealed in today's entrepreneurial age. We see new markets, new customer needs, new technologies, new social networking options generating opportunities at an explosive pace. And many new ventures are launched "entrepreneurially," with minimal resources, often even without a formal business plan. Emphasis is on generating revenue, "take a hill," see where we are, and then plan the next strategy. This often works, at least to start the business, and in today's changing markets, it is an excellent strategy.

Assuming you *do* get the startup funds and launch the business, odds are against you that you will succeed long term; more than half of these companies fail after the initial three years. Great product, great market, reasonable pricing, strong team—all the factors that would attract capital and you would think would drive success. So why so many failures, what is wrong here?

The real challenge comes next, moving from an entrepreneurial firm to what is often called a "professionally managed" firm,[29] enabling the company to attract growth capital (in contrast to seed or angel funding), attract a seasoned management team, and position the company for major value creation. The author's experience shows many of today's entrepreneurial managers often *do* have the critical skills needed—agility, adaptability and the requisite skills in finance, technology, marketing, and so on—but do not understand or ignore the *traditional* laws of management.

Let's look at one important traditional management tool, Porter's Five Forces Model, to answer the question, "Is this an attractive, growing market that will enable future profits to be achieved?"

Porter's Five Forces Model Measures Market Attractiveness

Porter's Five Forces Analysis, a deceptively simple, relatively easy to understand tool, provides insights on understanding market directions and attractiveness. Simply stated, if a market is highly competitive, may be impacted by substitute technologies, and is being "attacked" by new entrants seeking to capture market share ("attacked" is the right word here given what we see in many new Internet-based ventures), we can expect this market to be highly competitive with declining profit margins, and the market is considered "less attractive." By contrast, if the market is more stable, competition is minimal, and the impact of these market forces is less severe, we consider the market "attractive," capable of supporting higher profitability as demand develops. That summarizes the overall analysis here, and I find it is a helpful way to explain how the model is applied. Now let's take a deeper look at the process here. Keep in mind, as before, the planning process here is more important than the final answer on whether a market is "attractive" or "unattractive."

The Five Forces Model was developed in 1979 by a Harvard Business School professor, Michael Porter. It is hard for many to believe that a model developed more than three decades ago has relevance today. It does, and in some ways even more so. The Five Forces Model helps define whether a market is "attractive," meaning it can generate sustainable profit. Note the two key words here—"profit," not just sales revenue, and also "sustainable." To measure these, Porter's model looks at a sector, say Internet TV devices, and gauges how the following five forces impact this market sector:

- Threat of new entrants
- Threats from substitutes
- Degree of rivalry
- Bargaining power of buyers
- Bargaining power of suppliers[30]

Typically each force is ranked "low to high." If the overall analysis shows each of these forces are significant or "high," the market is expected to be highly competitive with price-cutting and low profitability; this is an "unattractive" market. Conversely, if these factors appear to be "insignificant," we anticipate higher sustainable profitability and the market appears "attractive."

For the proposed Jupiter product discussed earlier, the Five Forces analysis would identify a market in transition, with competition emerging from many sources, i.e., next generation network TVs (Philips has already announced a network TV product family), Internet services such as Hulu, Amazon Video on Demand, Xbox Video Marketplace, and others, driving down profitability, and creating the need for more funding. And these trends may have been missed in the business plan. What we are doing here is tempering the initial plan projections mentioned earlier about capturing "… 1 percent of a ten million household market," adding a dose of reality here. Properly done, showing this thinking early in the planning process sends a clear signal that the management team understands how their market dynamics and competitive landscape will shift over time. These are powerful insights that make a real difference when dealing with investors and other stakeholders.

How Traditional Management Tools Help Forge New Strategies

You also need to keep two other points in mind here. First, the planning *process* is important here. Concluding a market is "attractive" or "unattractive" is helpful, but *more* helpful is the process your team goes through to complete the analysis, i.e., understanding who the competition is today and in the future, what alternative technologies are emerging, to what extent will one or more large buyers or suppliers "own" the market, and so on. Again, the process here is really more important than the final answer, which is the same observation we have seen before.

Second, going through the above "threat of new entrants" planning process, you also identify specific issues and opportunities. For example, you may conclude that new competition for the Jupiter Model 2.0 is emerging from newspaper publishing-driven ventures that are also planning to offer access to Internet-based movies, a powerful integrated offering. What this suggests is you may want to pursue a new strategy—develop a strategic alliance with one or more major publishers to also offer news services. This was not part of your original plan, and maybe not even mentioned during the team's numerous technical meetings, but was developed using a *traditional* management tool to examine competitive market dynamics, Porter's Five Forces Model. Solid competitive and market dynamics analysis, not a founder's gut feel or "fingerspitzengefuhl" or the technology "gee whiz" factor, often drive strategy. And building in this thinking always creates a stronger plan; that is the key point here and a defensible winning approach based on my experience.

I have simplified the Five Forces Model Analysis, but the above does cover the essence of how this tool is applied and representative results of the planning process. Porter's Five Forces Model is a staple in business management courses—used with case analyses, this is an excellent tool to understand the strategy management process in both emerging ventures and major corporations.

Coca-Cola: How One Leading Edge Company Assesses Competition and Opportunities

The Five Forces analysis is a well-proven tool that, if properly applied, enhances performance and helps tighten business strategy. More insights on how early-stage firms can benefit can be shown looking at one leading edge beverage firm, Coca-Cola. Most are familiar with the "cola wars" with Pepsi and Coca-Cola battling in the cola market for share in stores, vending machines, and restaurants. Several well-known Harvard School Business cases address this topic, providing a powerful teaching tool used by the author and others.

My experience is competitive analysis, if properly applied within emerging firms, helps focus the business and enhance performance. To show how early-stage firms may benefit, let's look at how Coca-Cola, approaches the competitive analysis process.

Most business school students are familiar with the "cola wars" with Pepsi and Coca-Cola battling in the cola market for share in stores, vending machines, and restaurants. Intuitively most may view "cola" drinks as Coca-Cola's competition, a reasonable assumption. But Coca-Cola's management viewed noncarbonated beverages, or the NCB market, as their competition. Understanding that water, not necessarily Pepsi or other cola products, was their long-term competition, Coca-Cola moved into the bottled water business, which may seem surprising for a cola manufacturer. Coca Cola really created a *new* innovation staircase, demanding new strategies that may impact their current business. That is how a market leader handles competitive analysis to drive new strategies. Review any of the Harvard Business School case studies dealing with the cola wars, and you will clearly see the role the Porters Five Forces Analysis Model and other tools play here in defining the competitive landscape.[31]

Take a step back, and you see the thinking here. New entrants were meeting customers' needs and reshaping the traditional cola market. Coca-Cola responded by redefining a new target market. So given this definition of Coca-Cola's NCB market and growth targets, I would not be surprised to go to the supermarket someday and see milk branded by Coca-Cola. Milk branded by Coca-Cola?

It may sound strange now, but if you accept the above analysis, this is reasonable. Understanding where markets are heading and positioning to address these are traditional management skills employed by Coca-Cola, clearly a market leader. Today's entrepreneurial age management must also adapt and use these skills. The bad news—my experience suggests many emerging company management teams unfortunately fall short here. The good news—these skills can be learned.

SWOT analysis is another traditional management tool that, if properly applied, improves the defensibility of a business plan for both early-stage ventures as well as established companies. Let's take a closer look at the SWOT analysis, what it is, and how it is developed.

SWOT Analysis: A Closer Look—Understanding the Process

It is helpful to keep in mind the strategy management process most firms—both large and small—go through. As discussed before, market analysis and market share analysis projections are followed by competitive market analysis to define whether the company's target market is attractive—that is to say, will competitive intensity be manageable so the company can meet its revenue and earnings targets? That was the focus of the Porter's Five Forces Model discussed earlier.

The SWOT analysis builds on the Five Forces Model and looks at four factors:

o *Strengths:* company resources that support the ability to successfully meet business objectives
o *Weaknesses:* company resources that are lacking or other impediments that impact the ability to successfully meet business objectives
o *Opportunities:* external conditions that *enhance* the company's ability to successfully meet business objectives

o   *Threats:* external conditions that *impede* the company's ability to successfully meet business objectives

Looking at the above, you see strengths and weaknesses address *internal* factors, addressing the question: how well do my internal resources enable me to meet business objectives? By contrast, the two other factors, opportunities and threats, address *external* factors, addressing the question: to what extent do other situations, which may be directly or indirectly linked to our market, either enhance or possibly impact our business plan?

SWOT Analysis: A Strategy Development Tool Disguised as a Competitive Analysis Tool

I am exaggerating here to emphasize an important point that will be clear shortly. I sometimes, though not too often, see a business plan that includes a traditional SWOT analysis that may be quite detailed. At the end of the analysis, there may be words that summarize the analysis, maybe saying something like this: *The results of the SWOT analysis for the Auto Widget show our products are well positioned vs. the competition, we understand the threats and they present no problems, and we are well positioned to pursue new opportunities as they emerge.* This is a good high-level summary of the SWOT analysis from a competitive analysis perspective—it did its job here. Unfortunately, it really missed the mark in understanding how findings here help define company strategy.

Suppose for the Auto Widget, a hypothetical new plug-in car air freshener, the SWOT analysis identified the threat that auto manufacturers and third-party suppliers may offer similar products integrated with the car heaters and filters. And suppose a "strength" developed within the SWOT analysis is Auto Widget's patent for the mechanism used to select and deliver up to six different air freshener aromas from one device. One representative result of the SWOT analysis is a possible new strategy to develop a licensing program whereby Auto Widget's technology is licensed to auto manufacturers and aftermarket suppliers. What we are doing here is using the SWOT analysis as a strategy development tool, a very effective business planning technique. Fleshing out company strengths and using these to address opportunities, mitigate threats, and develop new strategies are the significant benefits here.

I have been involved in or led team sessions using this approach, creating a detailed SWOT and formulating possible strategies, and I find you need to encourage the planning team to brainstorm *all* strengths. A good starting framework for these discussions is to first broadly identify all company functions, e.g., production, logistics, sales, support, technology development, intellectual property, global locations, and so on. For each area, identify company strengths to the extent they exist. These ideas, which often may be pasted all over the wall, are distilled and summarized.

Next, the team looks at opportunities, posing the following question: *given the company's strengths and the opportunities we foresee here, what possible strategies should we pursue to meet our growth objectives?* You are creating possible strategies that ideally enable the company to meet its objectives. Next you look at, and rank threats, and develop possible strategies to mitigate the most significant threats. Creating "opportunity-driven" strategies, defended by a well thought out, defensible SWOT analysis, sends a powerful message that management understands the business and is well equipped to build a successful company. The team's entrepreneurial spirit and enthusiasm always play a key role, but the ability to use traditional management techniques to dissect business opportunities and create defensible strategies, I find, is even more important here.

In turnaround situations, where a company faces serious issues and threats, the process is reversed with *threats*, rather than *opportunities*, being the new strategy driver. Similar process, often more defensive than offensive, but the same objective here—optimize company positioning based on the SWOT analysis.

Walt Disney: How to Successfully Identify and Leverage Company Strengths

The Walt Disney Company is one excellent example I often use to show how understanding and leveraging corporate strengths drives successful strategies. In 1984, Michael Eisner was appointed CEO after four years of dismal financial returns. Disney was in trouble and needed a new strategy. Under Eisner's leadership, during the next four years Disney revenue increased from $1.66 billion to $3.75 billion, net profits increased from $98 million to $570 million, and its stock market valuation increased from $1.8 billion to $10.3 billion. So how did he do it? What strategies were pursued?

Eisner identified Disney's key strength as its film library, brand name, and animation skills and developed strategies to exploit these strengths. He released old Disney classics, started the Disney Channel, created films under the Touchstone label, and created major animation hits such as *The Little Mermaid* and others. Each of these and other related strategies leveraged Disney's intellectual property assets. Identifying what are the *most* leveragable corporate strengths and developing and executing successful strategies are what is needed to win. That is a traditional management process and Disney, under Eisner's leadership did it well.[32]

Today's competitive world is driven by rapid changes in technology, market segmentation, distribution channels, pricing, strategies, and positioning. Virtually every market sector is being attacked in today's global entrepreneurial market frenzy. Challenging existing markets and creating new ones are today's direction. The Laws of Management Strategy provide a place to stand and, if properly applied, provide a powerful management to develop successful strategies addressing both new opportunities and threats.

⚭

Chapter 12

Entrepreneurial "People" Management: Theory X and Theory Y—Schools of Management, Not Algebra

Management is nothing more than motivating other people.
Lee Iacocca

The People Motivation and Management Challenge

How do you manage and organize staff to maximize the performance and efficiency of the group? It seems like a simple question, but like many questions I shared with you, look deeper, and you realize answering this is tougher than it looks.

Suppose you work in a well-established company making automotive electronics systems and your main customers are auto manufacturers. You are a group manager with ten staff members. Your director requests a meeting with you and all your staff and says the following:

> *Our president yesterday advised all management staff that he wants to develop a new product to broaden our product line and enter the consumer automotive electronics market. He believes this will be an exciting product area that offers high potential for our company, and I agree. However, as you know, budgets are tight, so he emphasized that we can't add any new staff to develop this new business. I am counting on you all to pitch in here to help make this new business a success. This may mean extra hours and some personal sacrifices, but this is an exciting business area, a new frontier that I expect will offer you all many new career opportunities.*

So what is your reaction to the above? And what do you think will be the reaction of other staff members in your group? Representative comments from your staff may be as follows:

Fred: *"Is management kidding? I work ten hours a day now, rarely have dinner with my kids, and work during the weekend—no way I can do any more even if they give me a few more dollars a week or some perks."*

Mary: *"Sounds like it could be exciting, certainly better than the routine established products we are making now. I feel energized again, like the idea, look forward to hearing more about this—hope they give me some information to read."*

Jim: *"This sounds like more work. I work hard now and get a fair salary. If I do more work so the company doesn't have to hire more staff, I should get a raise—that is fair."*

Ellen: *"This sounds crazy—we are well established and known in our market for more than twenty years. We know this business. We don't know the consumer market. I see losses ahead, spending money here that will impact profits and my year-end bonus. Don't like this idea."*

John: *"I really like this idea, but too much negative thinking around me, afraid to do new things, very content doing yesterday's business. Good people, just not looking beyond today. Not sure I fit in with this group thinking here and see this as a real challenge."*

There are many variations on the above, but you get the point here. I am also sure you can relate to these reactions; most of us have seen these often. The above is obviously a simplification. If you study management and organizational behavior (usually called OB for short), you address the same questions dealing with thousands of diverse staff members involving all departments within a global organization. Further complicating the above are cultural differences that impact how groups are ideally structured and managed. Think about the planning factors that are involved in structuring and managing organizations—the mix of employee skills and capabilities, staff motivations, "who works well with whom," geography, productivity, work flows, efficiency, and many more.

The bottom line—pursuing new business ventures, moving from a mature, flat market to a high-growth market opportunity, often creates challenging "people" problems. And these problems emerge whether you have organizations with thousands of employees or a start-up working in a garage with a handful of people hoping to make their fortune with the next Internet startup.

So now go back to my initial question, how do you manage and organize staff to maximize the performance and efficiency of the group? Given the president's directive on the need to pursue new business and the mix of attitudes you see in your group, how do you organize and motivate your team? This really is more difficult than it looks. So how *do* you handle these issues? First, recognize there *are* tools and processes that help managers develop "winning" organizations—a tough task, but it can be done.

Organization management principles have evolved during the past centuries (that is right—centuries). Looking back, understanding why these changes occurred and their implications provides some insights on developing effective organizations to meet *today's* entrepreneurial age challenges. For our purposes here, I will cover what I believe are some key points you need to know. A good starting point is about 260 years ago, the birth of the Industrial Revolution.

Industrial Revolution: Machines Displace People and Change the Rules[33]

In the mid-1700s, the Industrial Revolution displaced workers with machines, creating new opportunities, increased productivity, and innovation. The steam engine and electricity were among the catalysts driving change in this era. But with these changes came the need to more efficiently manage people, resources, and money. The management challenge of motivating employees to work and maximizing productivity was much more complex than the simple traditional farming model driven by the simple rule, "Employees will always work hard to earn money."

Machines demanded processes that also more effectively managed time and decision making. In the farming model, communications delays and changes had minimal impact, but as machines and assembly lines emerged, we needed to improve our ability to adapt and optimize work processes. New structures and principles emerged, usually derived from military or religious organizations, to meet these challenges.

These sets of rules were usually referred to as "schools of management"—not really brick-and-mortar schools but really a collection of ideas that emerged to meet the changing management ground rules. While I am simplifying here, the basic question addressed by these new rules or schools of management was as follows:

> *Automation is changing the traditional farming model for workers. How do we structure organizations to both optimize productivity and profits, while ensuring we develop motivated and engaged workers that fully support company objectives?*

Over time, these schools of management evolved, and new ideas and rules emerged addressing this challenge. Proposed solutions varied widely but all tried, in their own way, to address this basic question. Keep this question in mind as we briefly review the schools of management evolution. And also keep in mind the evolution that is described below occurred over about a 150-year period. Compare that to today's changing people management challenge driven by rapidly accelerating technologies that only emerged during the past decade. We will discuss today's people management challenges shortly. First, lets have a brief history lesson on the 'schools of management" evolution.

The Schools of Management: From Therbligs to Theory X and Y and More

First the *scientific* management school emerged in the mid 1800s believing there was one best way to get a job done. To find this solution, you scientifically studied the people, processes, observe, analyze, and create new ideal procedures. Structure and hierarchy were important, so managers should *manage* and make decisions, while workers should *work*. Motivation was *not* important; people would work to earn money. Period.

In the early 1900s, scientific management was further refined by time and motion analysis, i.e., study the steps in each process and optimize processes to reduce motions, save time and thus reduce costs. Frank and Lillian Gilbreth, a leading husband-and-wife team and psychologists by training, took this one step further. They used time and motion studies to analyze hand movements, breaking down all tasks into a series of standard hand movements called "therbligs"—grabbing, searching, sorting, and other tasks could then be optimized examining units of therbligs, which incidentally was the Gilbreth's last name spelled backward. One often mentioned example using Gilbreth's ideas is in brick building construction. By measuring hand movements and motions to optimize stacking and laying bricks, bricklayer efficiency was almost tripled.[34]

It probably sounds foreign to many of today's knowledge economy workers measuring how much effort, measured in therbligs, it took to produce a product, but that was how it was done.

Next the *classical* school of management emerged, which primarily focused on increasing efficiency in larger organizations. Henri Fayol, a French engineer, played a role in this era, writing a classic management book, *General and Industrial Management*, where he suggested management performed five basic functions: planning, organizing, commanding, coordinating, and controlling. Fayol went on to define fourteen management principles including his famous "unity of command principle": *"For any action whatsoever, an employee should receive orders from one superior only."* Keep in mind this occurred in the 1920s and represented new management thinking at the time. In today's strategy management texts and courses, we typically define manager's responsibilities in four areas: planning, organizing, leading, and controlling. Evolution of this definition can be directly traced to Fayol's early work more than eighty years ago.[35]

Other thought leaders emerged to further refine the classical school of management ideas and processes. Max Weber, a German intellectual, is credited in the 1920s with developing processes to manage and control large organizations. Remember this was the era that large steel, oil, automotive, and other companies emerged, and they needed management help. Weber's model was to create an organization with a formal set of procedures and processes to support scalable operations, and he called this "bureaucracy." He did not envision red tape, but rather viewed bureaucracy as the most efficient form of organization having the following characteristics:

- A well-defined hierarchy of authority
- A clear division of work
- A system of rules covering the rights and duties of position incumbents
- A system of procedures for dealing with the work situation
- Impersonality of interpersonal relationships
- Selection for employment and promotion based on technical competence[36]

Again I am sure this sounds foreign to many in today's entrepreneurially driven, knowledge economy, but this was the environment in the 1920s and following years. What was missing from the above was any effort to really address worker motivation and job satisfaction. That was coming soon driven by lots of social changes, including the growth of unions, women's right to vote, and the general public's backlash to large business.

Responding to these and other changes, the *behavioral* school of management emerged. The Hawthorne Studies in the 1920s looked at assembly workers in a Western Electric plant. Their studies concluded that "social conditions of the workers, not just the working conditions, influenced behavior and performance at work." Prior to this study, the thinking was what employees earned, and the working conditions (e.g., start time, work environment, and so on) were the key drivers. Now a new element was introduced to optimize performance, the "needs and desires of the workers." Radical new thinking at the time and the start of the behavioral school of management.[37]

Let's look closer at one organizational management thinker at the time, Douglas McGregor, and his Theory X and Theory Y concepts, which I believe are relevant in today's entrepreneurial age organizations.

Balancing Performance and People Needs: Theory X and Theory Y

McGregor taught at the MIT in the late 1940s and early 1950s. Simply stated, McGregor believed that classical organizations, with highly centralized, tops-down decision making and specialized jobs, were really driven by basic assumptions about human behavior. He suggested there are two classes of assumptions about people, which he called *Theory X* and *Theory Y.*[38]

Most management thinking to that time was founded on what McGregor defined as Theory X assumptions about motivations and worker needs—workers dislike work and responsibility and prefer to be directed; workers are mainly motivated by financial rewards, not by the desire to do a good job; and given these observations, most workers must be closely managed, controlled, and rewarded to achieve company objectives.

Observing diversification and other market changes, McGregor suggested a new set of assumptions about worker motivations. Calling this *Theory X* and *Theory Y*, he suggested they provided a "blueprint" for management based on assumptions about human nature. *Theory X* assumed people dislike work and authority, need to be directed, are not concerned about job enrichment, and must be coerced to work. *Theory Y* held that people could enjoy work and be motivated; will self-control their performance if conditions are right; and people are motivated by the desire to do a good job rather than solely by financial rewards.[39]

It is surprising to many that this thinking emerged only about sixty years ago. Radical thinking at the time that was a real beachhead in the new *behavioral* school of management.

The Organizational Challenges for Today's High Growth Emerging Ventures

So looking at the above evolution of management thought during the past two centuries or so, what are the lessons here? What are recommendations for today's companies wrestling with one basic question?

> *How do we structure organizations to both optimize productivity and profits, while ensuring we develop motivated and engaged workers that fully support company objectives?*

This should look familiar; it is the same question posed earlier in the chapter and the same challenge faced by managers for centuries. What have we learned, and how do we address *today's* challenges?

Compounding today's management challenge is we are in the *entrepreneurial age,* where products may be a Web page, a virtual reality, a data-mining process, and other knowledge-based resources, where we measure mouse clicks, not *therbligs* or hand movements. And rapid product development and launch coupled with short product life cycles are the norm.

Clearly money alone does not motivate today's workers. Job content, interaction with peers and management, a positive corporate culture, company leadership—these and others are what motivate today's workers. And this suggests *Theory Y* thinking—that direction is what we expect today and that is what we see. On the surface, this is intuitively a good model to drive today's emerging firms. But emerging firms do need to be sensitive to some landmines here as well.

In today's highly collaborative, participatory management-driven companies, my experience suggests it is an easy and seductive trap for emerging firms to fall into employing a *Theory Y* approach too aggressively. Building a cooperative, friendly, easy-to-communicate-at-all-levels, "ping-pong-table-in-the corner" organization is a powerful tool to attract and motivate staff and compete in today's fast-paced markets. I use this approach myself with some ventures. What I am suggesting is the need for moving beyond the start-up phase, achieving growth, attracting new staff, building the infrastructure and auditable systems needed to attract capital, and so on. These needs demand a more *traditional* management approach with layered controls, processes, reporting with clearly defined structures. And yes, clearly defined goals for employees whereby compensation is based on performance and measured on how well personal goals are achieved. It starts to look like a *traditional* organization that, as it expands, may be driven by many *Theory X* principles. So the challenge is evolution, retaining the "ping-pong table-in-the-corner" spirit, but operating with a traditional management foundation. Not an easy task but it can be done.

And what about new ventures started within a major corporation that may have a traditional Theory X management culture? How do these ventures operate entrepreneurially, communicating a Theory Y message to attract talented staff, respond to market needs, and grow? Integrating Theory Y techniques is what is needed, and this is easier said than done in larger companies with well-established employee policies and compensation structures in place.

And that summarizes the real challenge here for developing responsive entrepreneurial organizations. To survive, grow, and attract capital, managers leading emerging ventures must understand and adopt traditional management tools and processes to grow. Having a ping-pong table in the corner may be great for morale, help creative juices flow, and attract staff, but traditional management principles are also essential. How to create these structures and processes given today's virtual, highly fragmented organizations is a real challenge.

And traditional firms seeking to pursue new ventures must also adopt entrepreneurial thinking to succeed. Creating the optimum organization to meet corporate objectives demands a change of thinking, often a difficult task.

Now let's take a look at the global market challenges for today's entrepreneurial age firms.

⚭

Chapter 13

Global Business: Why Pursue It, How It Works—the Story of Fred's Furniture Store

On The Need for Global Understanding ...

An Englishman, a Frenchman and a German were arguing about the respective merits of their language. The Frenchman was saying that French was the language of love, the language of romance, the most beautiful and pure language in the world. The German was asserting that German was the most vigorous language, the language of philosophers, the language of Goethe, the language most adaptable to the modern world of science and technology. When the Englishman's turn came, he said:

"I don't understand what you fellows are talking about. Take this (and he held up a table knife). You in France call it un couteau. You Germans call it ein Messer. We in England simply call it a knife, all said and done, is precisely what it is."

Lord Campbell of Askan, Chairman, Commonwealth Sugar Exporters' Association; Milton Keyes Development Corporation; Stateman Publishing Company[40]

Chapter 13?

Side Business: Why Pursue It, How It Works
Story of Red's Furniture Store

International Business Is Tough: Why Bother?

Working with many emerging firms, I am always surprised to hear questions such as "Why should we pursue international business? Given how tough it is, why don't we invest our resources here?" And the most often-repeated comment: "The U.S. is a major market—why bother looking at any international markets?" And I find many entry-level business school students have the same mindset, at least initially.

Teaching courses in strategy management, entrepreneurship, and international business, I also find students surprised about the realities of the global market, at least before taking the course. Misconceptions about the global market are widespread, and a major education gap exists here. Let me share some perspectives that hopefully will help.

We all look at the China and India export growth and their dominant share of the global market, and there are backlash grumblings about the need to "buy American." Later in this chapter, we will revisit the "buy American" issue. First, let's look at the *Forbes* ranking of Global 2000 firms, i.e., the two thousand largest companies in the world with global reach into all overseas markets. Suppose you add up revenues of Global 2000 companies by country where they are headquartered. Next look at the GDP of each of these countries and ask the question: what are the top three countries with the highest total Global 2000 revenue as a percent of GDP? Switzerland ranks highest at 245 percent, followed by the Netherlands at 218 percent, and the United Kingdom at 112 percent.

What countries do you think are the bottom three? China at 4, India at 5, and Mexico at 11 percent. Obviously the GDPs are higher in China and India, but this shows the impact of major *companies* in the global markets. Global *companies*, not *countries*, compete in global markets

In reality, understanding all aspects of global business—how it works, implications, strategies, opportunities, and looking beyond the hyperbole—is an essential business management skill. Look deeper at the today's changing global markets and statistics, and this will be clear.

Let's look at the Fortune 500 companies. I expect most readers, as with most students I encounter, are surprised to learn that more than 50 percent of Fortune 500 sales and earnings come from international business. My experience is most expect this to be less than 20 percent of sales. And this number has been increasing each year. Studies surveying Fortune 500 CEOs suggest most expect this trend to continue during the next five years. Examining the growth of one company, McDonald's, provides some insights here. In the early 1980s, McDonald's faced growth challenges with a maturing market and competition and decided to ramp up their global business. In 1980, 28 percent of new restaurants were overseas, and within ten years, more than *70 percent* of their new restaurants were located overseas. Why? Overseas markets provided strong upside—in the United States, there was one restaurant per twenty-five thousand people compared to one per five hundred thousand people in overseas markets.[41] Today almost 70 percent of McDonald's revenue and more then half its profits come from overseas.

So in the case of the fast food market, McDonalds was able to export its *widely accepted products and highly efficient processes* to compete in new markets and achieve sales growth. The assumption is what works in the U.S. market can be exported to pursue similar opportunities in an overseas market. Whether you are McDonald's selling fast food, Proctor and Gamble selling soap, or Kellogg's selling cereal, the strategy is do overseas what you do efficiently here and increase sales and profits. Working through the process is a bit more complicated, but this is the general idea.

Achieving critical mass is the driver for most players. So whether you sell hamburgers, soap, or software systems, ideally you want to sell *exactly* the same product anywhere on the planet. No modifications, no extra cost, no change in business processes—that is the ideal situation providing two benefits:

- Access to new markets, moving beyond often saturated local markets increases revenues

Think soap here. Large factory in the United States making soap bars. Company has strong market share in all U.S. markets, but sales are flat. Just like the McDonald's example, the company needs more customers to sell to.

- Increasing production levels usually enables greater production efficiencies and lowers per unit costs.

Several effects are at work here. Buying larger quantities of raw materials lowers per unit costs and increases profits for *all* sales, both international and domestic. This is a key point. Second, make more of a given product and the effects of both the learning curve (per unit costs drop as companies learn more efficient ways to manufacture) and experience curve (per unit costs drop further due to total accumulated production) further drive down costs.

The benefits of "going global" are clear—increased sales, lower per unit costs, and thus create increased profits. And this is what drives companies to pursue global business. Achieving this objective is not as simple as it seems, however, as any experienced global executive or business school student will tell you. Look closer at the international market and you realize the magnitude of the challenges and strategic choices you need to address. Let's look at some of the potholes often encountered on the road to building a global business.

Potholes on the Road to Creating a Global Business: Markets, Products, Manufacturing

First, all markets are not equal. There is no ubiquitous global market. Take soap for example. It may look like one product fits all markets, but it doesn't. Different markets have diverse preferences in soap smell, color, shape, and the advertising message used to position and sell the product in global markets.

Second, staying with our soap example, suppose you understand the market nuances, and you are asked to develop the company's global strategy. You have done your market analysis homework, and you recommend a new soap product customized for overseas markets.

You need to decide where you manufacture these "customized" products. Remember your U.S. production facility is efficient, very efficient, making soap bars for U.S. customers. And remember the benefits of going global—make more of the same product, lower per unit costs, increase profits. Now you are recommending that management change these highly efficient production facilities to create customized products with lower production runs, new added costs for equipment modifications, product labeling, training, and so on. No ubiquitous global product here, and this is the same story for almost all products and many services as well. Tastes, preferences, cultural sensitivities, needs vary among countries. Keep in mind the initial assumption here: global business will *increase* revenue and profits. Looks like you have a dilemma here.

Next, remember if your U.S. production facility is in Atlanta, you can efficiently reach and serve all U.S. markets. But say you now want to use this same facility to serve Japan, a new target global market. Shipping and related overhead costs may make this prohibitive.

Suppose you do establish an overseas entity, ensuring a reliable supplier and support may be a real challenge in some markets.

And keep in mind the cultural and language challenges and sensitivities. I shared some insights related to one of my many experiences in Japan in chapter 6. And we can cite many other issues encountered by major players seeking to export either well-known brands or well-proven, successful business processes to overseas markets. Some examples:[42]

- Pepsi's "Come Alive with the Pepsi Generation" was translated to "Pepsi will bring you ancestors back from the dead" in Taiwan.
- Coors used its slogan "Turn it Loose" to sell beer in Spain and Latin America, which was translated to "suffer from diarrhea."
- Frank Perdue's famous slogan, "It takes a tough man to make a tender chicken," was translated in Spanish into "It takes a sexually stimulated man to make a chicken affectionate."
- Electrolux, a Swedish company, entered the U.S. market with the following marketing slogan, "Nothing sucks like an Electrolux," clearly sending an unintended message.

Understanding global business planning, strategy development, protection of intellectual property, financials, and strategy execution is complex, make no mistake about it. Given its importance, I recommend that if you can, you take a course addressing global business, ideally one that integrates case studies showing best practices. One Harvard Business School case study I often use, for example, reviews GE's Medical Services division (GEMS) strategy for entering the China market.[43] Examining the issues here—strategic pricing, intellectual property protection, implementation and support issues, showing how a leading multinational firm creates value in diverse markets—provides an excellent learning experience helping understand global market challenges and best practices.

Summarizing, the two key issues here are the extent to which products must be customized to meet local needs and the extent to which companies must invest to develop overseas facilities, including production, engineering, marketing, support, and sales organization. How these fundamental issues are addressed forms the basis for a company's global business strategy, and this applies to Fortune 500 companies as well as emerging entrepreneurial firms who often face the same challenges. We will review this point further when we discuss "Fred's Furniture Store" shortly. First, we will review the typical strategic roadmap companies follow to pursue global business, and also explore the "buying American product" myth.

Strategic Roadmaps for Pursuing Global Business

While an in-depth review of global business is beyond the scope of *Chopstick*, I do want to briefly review two basic strategic roadmaps for creating global companies. Given the above background, I think these should be clear. Consider the following two types of corporate structures and how and when they may be used:[44]

- *Global company*—serves markets where global standards exist, governments don't prohibit imports, and there are significant production economies of scale. No significant customization is needed to meet market needs or local preferences. Here you would expect to keep all decision making and production centralized at headquarters with minimal autonomy and control by the local overseas division. Commodity products, components, and similar standardized, high-volume products are representative here.
- *Multinational company*—serves markets where local tastes and preferences drive the buying decision, governments may impose the mandate specifying required target levels of local labor content, and transportation costs may be high. Here you would expect many of the traditional headquarters functions and production to be replicated, with significant decision making and management control ceded to the local in-country division. A very different business structure from a *global* company—think

about the organizational and management challenges, the cross-cultural issues, the need to develop and create low-cost overseas production facilities and logistics processes, the need to develop a seamless global information system. These and many more challenges must be addressed to develop a successful global multinational company. Representative products here may be toothpaste, soap, breakfast cereals.

Other global business strategy roadmaps exist, typically showing a mix of the above, or perhaps decentralizing only certain functions, maybe using regional production centers to serve multiple overseas markets. What I have shared with you shows the basic global corporate structures and their key features. Keep in mind that for Fortune 500 firms, structuring and executing a successful global strategy to optimize revenue growth and profitability is a complex and daunting challenge.

Working with a major global pharmaceutical firm client some years ago, our team assisted in developing the global information architecture to support their diversified global business. Highlights of their business demonstrates the complexity and scale of the challenges here: offered both pharmaceutical and consumer drug products; more than 1,500 global locations; significant local market customization; decentralized global management structure; regional production and logistics facilities; global sourcing of raw materials to optimize raw material purchases to secure lowest prices based on currency fluctuations and country sales outlooks.

The Misconception of Buying American Products

Today we see a backlash toward foreign firms. Response of many to the explosive growth of international competition is " we need to 'buy American.'" And this is often heard from political leaders who should know this is misleading. And why is this so? Well, the first issue is to define exactly what is an "American product."

For example, to minimize cost and ensure the highest quality, many U.S. firms often establish a network of global suppliers for products manufactured in the United States. For example, look at the Boeing 777 commercial airliner, clearly a well-known American product. Well, sort of. The Boeing 777 has 3 million parts with 132,500 individual designed parts made by 545 suppliers, with 487 in the United States and 58 suppliers in a dozen other countries. Using "best of breed" global suppliers enables Boeing to create the highest-quality product at lowest cost.[45]

Now suppose you are heading home and have to stop at the store to pick up a few items. You are firmly committed to buying American. Here is a possible scenario:

> You stop at the local 7-11 to avoid a long supermarket check-out line. Pick up some beer—no German beer, you buy "all-American" Budweiser. Your dog needs food so you buy a ten-pound bag of Purina Dog Chow. Your baby needs some Gerber creamy vegetables and some Vaseline for a rash, and these go into the basket. Your wife said not to forget the mayonnaise, so you buy a small jar of Hellman's mayo. Last but not least, dessert, and you see Ben & Jerry's and Good Humor in the freezer. Thinking of the ice cream truck and the ringing bells going through your old neighborhood, a true "American" image, a package of Good Humor chocolate chip bars goes in the basket. Check out time—you pay, leave the store, and feel you have, in your own small way, "bought American" and helped keep jobs in your own turf. Well, not exactly. Let's take a closer look here:

- Budweiser, started in 1876, the "Great American Lager," is owned by Anheuser-Busch InBev, N.V. based in Leuven, Belgium.

- Purina, founded in 1894, is owned by Nestle Company in Switzerland. If you also had to pick up Friskies cat food for your cat, Nestle also owns that company as well.
- Gerber, founded in 1927, holds more than 80 percent of the U.S. baby food market and is owned by Novartis, a major Swiss pharmaceutical firm.
- Vaseline, developed in 1872, was acquired by the British/Dutch conglomerate Unilever, N.V.
- Hellman's, started with a recipe developed by a New York City deli owner in 1905, was purchased by Unilever in 2000.
- Good Humor is also owned by Unilever.

Not doing so well in "buying American," batting zero here. And suppose you bought the Ben & Jerry's instead of Good Humor? That wouldn't help much either since Ben & Jerry's, founded in 1978 in Vermont, is also owned by Unilever. But your effort to "buy American" was really doomed from the moment you entered the store since the entire 7-11 retail chain is owned by Seven & I Holdings Co., Ltd. in Japan, which owns about thirty-five thousand stores in approximately one hundred countries.[46]

While jobs in manufacturing and other key sectors are being exported with disastrous impact in many U.S. cities and small towns, the amount of foreign direct investment in the United States has, in fact, accelerated for a number of reasons including our declining dollar. That makes U.S. investments look highly attractive, and we can expect accelerated interest by major overseas players in buying major U.S. brands to expand their global market reach and directly enter the U.S. market.

Fred's Furniture Store: The Seductiveness of Global Business

I often share the story of Fred's Furniture, a Virginia-based manufacturer of high-end, custom-crafted hardwood tables and how Fred explores and enters the global marketplace. I developed this fictitious company model, and I find it effectively illustrates global business issues, strategies, opportunities, and new directions in today's entrepreneurial age driven global marketplace. Hopefully you will agree.

Fred Fudder makes tables. Great tables. Handcrafted, all wood, real fine furniture, Fred has been making his crafted tables for twenty years now, done reasonably well creating a lifestyle business, but changes are coming and Fred is concerned.

Let's look closer here at Fred's business. Fred's tables are simple. Four turned wooden legs. An "Americana" historical logo is wood burned onto the base of each leg—a unique branding idea conceived by Fred about ten years ago that helped build product awareness, Fred's brand, and sales.

The four legs are attached to a round solid wood tabletop offered in one size—thirty-six inches diameter. A simple product line and business model here—just a few parts, one table model, and Fred has created a profitable business.

Now let's look at the numbers here. Tables sell for $60 to retailers. They sell the tables retail for $100. Fred gets the four legs premanufactured and prefinished. He adds a lacquer finish and burns in the logo. Total labor and materials cost Fred $30 per table. Summarizing, Fred sells the table to retailers for $60, material and labor costs $30, so Fred makes $30 gross profit on each table he sells.

Fred sells about 2,500 tables a month or 30,000 tables a year so gross annual sales are $180,000, which provides $90,000 gross profit. Fred's overhead costs are about 25 percent of sales or $45,000 per year. Thus overall net profit for the business is $45,000 (gross profit less total overhead). A net profit of 25 percent of sales is respectable.

But Fred is worried. Other competitors now offer similar tables selling retail at $60 to $80 or sometimes even less. Quality may not be the same, and some are clearly "knock offs," but they are selling. Demand is being fueled by lower price.

Fred is also concerned about his increasing costs. Costs for the leg assemblies and hardware are creeping up, and he feels locked in buying small quantities from one supplier. Rising costs coupled with retail price reductions shrink profits. This is not a good situation, and Fred should be concerned.

Fred has a possible solution—go global. Maybe not sell to the entire planet, but focus on several high-potential target markets with customers who want to buy high-quality crafted tables. Maybe find some new markets, increase revenues, and with increased production volumes, be able to reduce material and assembly costs. This sounds like a good strategy.

Fred's thinking: first target the United Kingdom and Europe, who he thinks will be attracted to both the "Americana" branding and product quality. Helped by the Department of Commerce, always anxious to help small firms sell to the world, Fred starts with the United Kingdom and secures an international distributor. He ships his finished tables to the distributor, and they send Fred's tables to their local in-country retail stores. Initial sales go well, and the distributor adds France, Germany, and Belgium to broaden the market.

The numbers look good. International sales are ramping up to about five hundred tables a month and growing. Added to current business, Fred is now selling three thousand tables monthly. Business is going in the right direction.

Looking closer at the numbers, international business does add overhead cost of about 5 percent, now increasing from 25 to

30 percent of sales, Fred sells tables to overseas distributors at $50, which is $10 less than his price to U.S. distributors. Overseas retailers sell the tables at $120, which provides sufficient profit margins for overseas distributors and retailers.

Summarizing here, Fred is selling the same tables both overseas and in the United States. New overseas sales increase revenues and lower costs per table. The additional overhead is minimal and easily absorbed. Going global was a good idea, concludes Fred.

Fred sees the upside here, and to meet demand, Fred has ramped up production. He likes the idea of selling the same product in new global markets. Get the formula and business model right here, sell more overseas, and further reduce costs at his factory. It's a good strategy, and it works, for a while anyway.

Fred is now comfortable with his increased overhead to support global sales, but now sees some warning signs emerging. First, he sees new competition. The same competitors he is facing in the United States are now competing with him in his overseas markets. And rather than ship completed tables from their U.S. headquarters location, they set up a light assembly operation in each country. They ship parts into the country and use low-cost labor to assemble the finished products. Very little value-added in-country, just assembly. Why bother doing this? One reason is competitors may secure local benefits, e.g., possible tax and business development incentives offered by local government; support offering exposure to retail stores and the public—really free advertising, and other no-cost support.

Most important, the competitors' strategy lowers their costs in two ways. First, they sell more tables and thus buy materials in higher quantities and at lower costs—the same economies Fred was hoping to exploit. Second, their overhead costs may be less due to the local in-country incentives mentioned before and lower shipping costs. Having a lower cost means competitors can lower their prices, which is exactly what they do. Why? To capture additional market share, increase sales, and create further cost economies to increase profits. And that trend accelerates.

So now back to Fred. He wants the increased sales and sees the global opportunity, but he sees the threat. What should he do now?

Fred decides to match the competition. He sets up a modest assembly operation in his two main overseas markets, the United Kingdom and Belgium, loosely following his competitors' model. The one-time cost here mostly wipes out his annual profits, but he is investing in Fred's Furniture.

So business proceeds. Retail prices drop further, but with reduced assembly costs, Fred can still keep profits strong. There is great leverage selling the same "widget" or product globally; the economies of mass production kick in as global business accelerates. At least that is how is supposed to work. Fred now starts to see new warning signs emerge.

Retailers in Belgium want to see a new twenty-four-inch table and also want to offer a new style tabletop finished with gold trim. And the major national retailer in Spain, suggesting large sales volumes, really likes the product and will sell it, but wants to add a mosaic design tabletop. What is happening here?

Fred is encountering the same challenge every major firm faces when "going global." You may have a great product that sells well in the United States. You want to "go down the experience curve" and lower material cost by selling the *same* product overseas. But market conditions, sales channel partners, local customer preferences, competition, and sometimes even local governments force you to *customize* your product to meet local needs. You may think you have a global strategy, but often have to adapt to meet local market needs. The results are increased costs, usually lower profits, initially anyway, and a more complex management challenge.

Remember where Fred started here: putting assembled standard, "one size fits all" tables in a box and shipping them to an overseas distributor. Very simple model here. What we are talking about now is much more complicated, and more risky.

So what should Fred do now? Step back and you really see two options here. First, he can recognize "going global" is more complex than he thought and continue to operate a modest international business in several markets. Maybe he could offer a customized product in these markets. It may be lower profitability than U.S. sales, but with this option, he won't be "betting the farm" to chase global business, which will require significant investment.

Fred wants to make no more investment in his "going global" strategy. He understands he is missing other global business but now wants to limit his exposure, and that is what he chooses to do. So what is the result of Fred Furniture's global business expansion? Some increased sales, lower material costs, higher average overhead costs due to overseas operations, lower net profit from overseas sales, and maybe marginal change in overall profits. But Fred did gain access to new markets, expanded sales, and lowered material costs, gained experience in developing new products, gained understanding of how to access and sell to overseas customers— overall a good learning experience.

But suppose Fred had elected to go for it and *aggressively* pursue a global strategy. What would be the vision here? He would be following the same global business "blueprint" used by almost all firms that have created major lines of global business. There are some differences for products vs. services, and commodity vs. specialized products, but strategies are surprisingly similar. While high level, the following summarizes some key strategy options and issues related to "going global" strategies:

- Sell the same products in all overseas markets, or at least try to, just like Fred did.

- Sell customized products to meet local needs to capture market share. The tricky part is where do you *make* the basic products and where do you *customize* products to meet local needs.
- Set up manufacturing in each country to build products meeting local needs. Or you can consolidate manufacturing in one country, achieve economies of scale, ship components to local manufacturing, and assemble customized products. Or you can just set up sales offices in each country and make *all* global products in regional manufacturing centers.
- You see one key global strategy issue here. Where do you locate manufacturing to minimize costs and maximize market penetration in overseas markets?
- Other headquarters functions—engineering, logistics, and all support functions, such as human resources, finance, and marketing, are also needed to support Fred's overseas operations. Should you keep all these functions centralized at headquarters, moved to regional locations, or perhaps be fully replicated in each country?

I have greatly simplified the above for the Fred's Furniture example to illustrate the key *going global* points—addressing the above and the many other related "going global" issues is a challenge. But the global market offers exciting opportunities for emerging firms, and for Fortune 500 companies, it accounts for more than 50 percent of revenue. Understanding global business strategies and market trends, therefore, is a critically important skill that should be acquired by both entry-level as well as senior management staff.

Chapter 14

Metaphors and Models: Straw Men Do More than Chase the Birds Away and Walk with Tin Men and Lions

*Opportunity is often missed by most people because
it is dressed in overalls and looks like work.*
Thomas A. Edison

The Need for Metaphors and Models

During a senior college level entrepreneurship class I taught at a leading university, I assigned a student to develop a business model and straw man analysis for a new venture. The next day she asked to meet. She was a strong student, high GPA, smart, and well equipped to analyze business models and projections. But she told me she did not understand how to *develop* these projections; she had never learned these skills. *Analyzing* business models and *developing* new venture business models are not the same. This is a critical distinction that we will discuss further here.

We all crave models and metaphors to help reduce the complex to simple, understandable concepts. Models and metaphors help us deal with a rapidly changing world, driven by explosive changes in technology, markets, perspectives, politics, social relationships. Straw man models provide a starting point, a framework, to help us understand and dissect these changes.

Look at some of the "hard" changes—powerful low-cost computers, social networking, mobile applications, GPS, and many others. And the "soft" changes—moving to impersonal communications via computer screens, technical savvy four-year-olds' text messaging, and markets being reshaped so quickly we are hard pressed to understand or even define them.

So how do you develop, define, and secure support for new ventures given this changing market landscape? You need to develop skills to translate the abstract to more concrete concepts; models and metaphors help here. For example, only a few years ago, we talked about downloading and reading books on PCs. As mobile devices proliferated, we initially provided access to books, what we viewed as "traditional" books, via these devices. Now we created a new product class, called "e-books," which is a metaphor for a new class of products created solely to be read using "e-book readers." We can talk about books for specific mobile readers, but the metaphor here is e-book, which is now widely understood as a new product class.

Another example is the ATM. We all know what ATM means, and some are familiar with the complexities of clearinghouse and other systems that support this simple, widely accepted metaphor for electronic banking. Let's look at the thought process in developing a new venture in the mobile ATM arena to understand the issues here.

The Straw Man Process: Developing a New Mobile ATM Service—"Virtual Cash Pouch"

Suppose you are looking at a new wireless device service to securely move and manage your funds. For discussion here, it really makes no difference if you are looking at this from the perspective of an employee in a major corporation looking at entering a new business, a group of entrepreneurs "in a garage" whiteboarding a new venture, or a student asked to conceptualize a potential new venture in an entrepreneurship class. Similar thought process here for all. Key point—how you define this venture sends a message to many audiences, probably more than most realize, and can play a critical role in the venture's perception and support. This does take some thought to get it right.

So going back to our ATM example, suppose I view this as a "mobile ATM service," same functionality as an ATM, but mobile. Maybe I don't have cash in my hand, but the service could instantly credit funds to a branded debit card I carry in my wallet to make immediate funds available. This sends a signal that the new service competes with, and offers an alternative to, traditional ATM services. The advantages: we can define and quantify the ATM market; a baseline fee structure exists that we can use to develop our competitive pricing metrics, and we understand who the players are today and have some ideas on where this market is headed. The disadvantages: we are linking this to *yesterday's* market—ATM or "automated teller machines"—sort of sounds like NCR too tightly linking themselves to the market that defined their name National Cash Register Company. Other disadvantages: the ATM linkage is not emphasizing the "untethered" features offered by mobile services; we are positioning this as a mobile alternative to ATM services, but today's users seek enhanced, more full-featured services, for example, integrating financial management, budgeting, and other services.

Let's continue with the mobile ATM example and position the new venture as "Virtual Cash Pouch," a new mobile service competing in the emerging mobile cash payment and financial services markets. As mentioned earlier, these services are much further developed in overseas markets, such as Korea, but are in their infancy in the United States. So we now have a working name "Virtual Cash Pouch," and suppose we define VCP's scope of services as offering cash management, wireless retail payments, and access to integrated cash budgeting and management tools, maybe providing alerts to your mobile device showing when you are close to exceeding budget limits say for restaurant expenses or new clothes—you get the idea here.

So what this now looks like is a mobile payment and cash management system, going well beyond a mobile ATM service: new market, addresses several sectors, offers new capabilities such as "beaming" wireless payments to cashiers at restaurants and stores—no more card swipes. Summarizing, VCP competes in the new market for what I may call Virtual Mobile Cash Management Services (VMCM) that will offer users new ways to dramatically improve their cash management, improve budgeting, improve the vendor cash payment process, reduce costs, incentivize retailers to possibly offer discounts for "beamed" wireless payments.

What we accomplished above is to develop a model for a new market that I defined as VMCM, and defined a new venture, "Virtual Cash Pouch," which will offer a range of targeted services to compete in this market. Note we started with a broad service concepts, explored the benefits from the *user* perspective, and conceptualized a possible new product and its positioning. We defined the market where VCP will compete and discussed its key features. Navigating through the above process takes some experience but can be learned as I have seen often in many diverse environments.

The challenges based on the above should be clear. If you relate the new venture to a *traditional* business, you have a starting point to help define markets, scale, competition, critical success factors, financial metrics. If you position the venture as a *new* service, maybe a major innovation, you have many benefits, such as "first mover advantage," but you have to convince users, investors, and your team that a significant market exists, you have the ideal strategy to win, you have a competitive pricing strategy, and you are creating a sustainable, competitive business here.

I simplified the above, and there would usually be many iterations of alternative or "straw man" market models; the suggested Virtual Mobile Cash Management Services (VMCM) model may be the final selection after much discussion and formal review. Remember though the starting point here may have been a blank whiteboard, an idea for a new product or service, your task is to define a sustainable, competitive business.

Look at every sector and you see new products and services. You can expect to see an "alphabet soup" of metaphors as new markets emerge and traditional business evolves. Straw man business models provide the blueprint, enabling an easily understood business concept to be developed and shared. For example, many have heard the term "hub and spoke" network. That is the metaphor Fred Smith, founder of Federal Express, used to describe the company's business model, emphasize benefits, and explain the FedEx model to investors and the public. All other services up to that time shipped directly location to location if they were on the same or close spokes. The FedEx model required that all products are sent to the hub and resent—presumably more efficient, faster and lower cost. This was counterintuitive to many, but the "hub and spoke" term proved to be a powerful FedEx metaphor and insightful model that worked well to emphasize key benefits and explain the FedEx business model.

Years ago, I was involved in developing a new nationwide high-speed data network that rapidly routed data "packets" through global data nodes. Describing the new network as a "hot potato network" enabled many key new benefits to be emphasized—nodes quickly passed the data packets like "hot potatoes." Each packet was standardized, same size and shape like a potato; nodes were efficiently designed for a single function—move "hot potato" data packets and move them quickly. While this may seem simplistic, talking about potatoes moving around a network, there is an elegance here using a simple metaphor to create understanding among employees, investors, and third parties for an abstract new business concept, such as moving packets of bits.

Sometimes even animal metaphors are helpful to describe evolving markets, and camels are often my choice with the "camel-back" effect. For example, a profitable product is developed for a well-defined "single hump" market. But entrepreneurial age market forces and customer demand create a "two hump" market. Maybe only a high-end product was offered like an iPod, and then the market also demands a low-end product, like a Nano. Sometimes the market evolves quickly, very quickly for today's software products, into three or more market segments. While there may be a three-hump camel, it is more important to understand the analogy than worry about the animal in this case.

New Developments in Health Care: Emerging Models and Metaphors

In the biomedical market for example, I served as an advisor to an early-stage company forging new gene-based biomedical solutions to fight today's most challenging diseases. Biological "pathways" or "biomarkers" help genes, molecules, and cells communicate and offer exciting new opportunities to forge new solutions addressing today's most critical diseases. While some of these biomarkers have already been discovered, it is estimated today we have only "mapped" about 5 percent of all biomarkers, many of which may hold the key to creating dramatic new disease-fighting solutions. By understanding a patient's genetic biomarkers, determined by a spectral analysis of body fluids and other patient data, and using powerful advanced computing and analytic tools analyzing millions of biomarkers and traditional disease indicators, we can identify disease "predispositions," or the likelihood an individual will get a disease.

But we can go further. We can use this same data, a patient's unique molecular signature, to develop patient-specific drug treatments. For a breast cancer patient, as an example, that means identifying what is the optimum drug to prescribe, the recommended chemotherapy protocol—type, dosage, frequency, and, even more significant, whether chemotherapy should even be recommended based on the patient's unique "molecular signature." This is the age of "personalized medicine," the new market emerging to describe these new solutions.

Major pharmaceutical firms, research institutions, and many new ventures are entering this exciting market. Most would agree that these new solutions have the potential to dramatically reshape the traditional health care market, providing the opportunity to reduce both mortality and morbidity rates (roughly translated as the pain and mental suffering patients endure due to treatments).

These promising technical developments are coming. They are truly exciting, and I and many others believe they will radically reshape and improve today's health care system. But how do these new technical and research directions translate into changing industry and business structures? Significant new investment will be needed to launch and grow new businesses in these areas, but exactly where does it go? Saying this another way, what are the new straw man business models emerging here? Will they be research companies licensing technology, new product ventures, new health care service ventures, maybe joint ventures with other sectors?

This last point may sound far-fetched, but look at one example—we are now seeing "smart garments," which can track your vital signs and gauge your health status. As mentioned earlier in *Chopstick*, I would not be surprised to see a "health jacket" using this technology, perhaps offered in Nordstrom's, developed as a joint venture with a health care company. Choosing a health care monitoring device off a clothing rack in a department store may sound far out. But just like the wireless pills I mentioned early in *Chopstick*, these are coming and quickly.

Dissecting these market and technology changes and defining potential new business opportunities are challenges for both major players and emerging firms. Straw man models provide an effective tool to meet this need.

Guidelines for the Straw Man Modeling Process

Process is the key word here. While straw man models help define possible business structures, more important is understanding how you get there. The team's thought processes and interaction, the fleshing out of alternatives, the analysis of tradeoffs, risks and opportunities—these are the *real* benefits of the process. To again quote General and former President Eisenhower, *"The plan is nothing; the planning process is everything."*

Overemphasized perhaps, but it did work for the D-Day invasion plan, and I think it provides good counsel for the straw man planning process as well.

The straw man planning process needs to capture diverse inputs. While all organizations have smart, highly talented staff, creating straw man models works best as a team-driven experience.

Intellectual leaders in an organization can and should play a role here, but there is great value in using a "bottoms-up" approach to develop and capture new business ideas.

Keep in mind a straw man model is appropriately named. After it is created, the team's job is, as I often say, "to knock the stuffing out of it." The main point here—and it is an important one—is conceptualizing "straw man" models and sharing these, rather than *completed* business models, with your planning staff creates a more motivated, engaged team. I use this approach often, and it is highly recommended.

You recall the discussion related to the Jupiter Model 2.0 Internet video device we discussed in chapter 2 and my questions drilling down on the business model details. While the Jupiter team generally understood the possibilities, they clearly did not examine all the business tradeoffs and implications—is this a service, product, or licensing business model: what are the tradeoffs here; what would be the structure of a Jupiter service business; and so on? All these and others could have been addressed if the Jupiter management team and staff worked through the straw man modeling process and fleshed out the details. There are many types of straw man models and many ways to create them. Let me give you an example how this might work.

Suppose the Jupiter management team leads a planning meeting with the objective of developing straw man business models Jupiter can pursue, emphasizing they want to capture *all* the ideas of the staff and draw on their experience base. As a start, a facilitator, who can be a senior executive or a consultant, starts the session perhaps suggesting two initial classes of "straw man" opportunities, broadly grouped into products and services. With this starting point, and two large blank whiteboards, one with *products* and one with *services* marked on top, attendees are asked to propose ideas in either *bucket*. It can be a far out or conservative idea—it doesn't matter. This is a brainstorming session, and you are just identifying possibilities. The ideas are written on the board or pasted on the walls. After the initial pass, if you have a creative, energized team, all the walls may be covered.

After this initial session, I usually pursue two alternative approaches if I am *guiding* the discussion. *Guiding* is the proper word here. If you are leading a company, you need to stay back to ensure you capture your team's thinking and ideas. In emerging firms, I find this is often a problem for a strong founding CEO. Nonetheless, this is a valuable management skill to develop, and like many disciplines discussed in *Chopstick*, it can be learned. Back to our planning session, let's look at possible next steps here. Suppose one straw man service concept looked particularly innovative and promising. The facilitator would paste this on the board and ask discussion questions soliciting comments about external and internal factors, possible strategies, pricing metrics, target customers, demographics, and other information. Where possible, the discussion would capture the thought process here—*why* a specific recommendation was suggested. Properly done, this structured process identifies possibilities. Possibilities are translated into straw man models that define potential business opportunities. I left out some details here, such as the need to initially provide background materials to all participants, but I think you get the point here.

And you definitely need to "think out of the room" as discussed earlier. Good counsel to work on developing this skill, and straw man sessions are a good place to start.

So going back to our health care market example, what are some ideas, possible straw man models that emerge, "thinking out of the room," going through this process? Here are some possibilities that illustrate the process:

• New medical service firms offering, maybe for $49.95, to develop your molecular signature and determine what diseases you are most likely to develop, what preventative, diet, or nutritional protocols are recommended to improve your health based on your unique profile. Medical services firms are loosely defined here and may not be what you view as medical companies today since these may be "analysis" services not "medical" services. Maybe, maybe not. How we bound our straw man model in this case defines whether these services are only offered by traditional certified health care providers or are offered perhaps in convenience stores purchased off a rack much like a prepaid cellular phone. "Molecular Signature Health Analysis in a Box" may be coming to a store near you, hopefully with a catchier product name than I show here. So if you are a major health care player and plan on entering what you feel is a major market, which I believe it is, the straw man modeling process helps you define the competitive landscape and whom you may be competing with. That is why I emphasize that internalizing the straw man modeling process helps managers better understand market dynamics in relatively undefined markets.

- New medical audit firms may emerge that will, for a fee, "audit" prescribed medical treatments to provide a second opinion on a patient's treatment and prognosis. Second opinions may be "molecular signature" based, coupled with patient's vital signs and prior diagnoses. And I expect nutritional supplement firms, as a complementary service, may assess current patient condition and health outlook and propose a recommended "personalized" supplement regimen to optimize a patient's health and wellness. Helping drive these new services is our improved ability to access and share patient medical records with the emergence of new Electronic Health Record standards and new "Blue Button" services recently proposed by President Obama. Depressing one "Blue Button" will, as the services develop, provide users with the ability to share all personal health care records with third parties. Eliminating "sneaker-net" to move records from multiple medical facilities, ease of sharing records quickly with third parties, and exciting new molecular signature technologies are some trends driving the straw man models emerging in the health care arena.

While the straw man model defines the new business, this is a high-level analysis, and many questions remain—i.e., what if any regulations will govern these services; to what extent will overseas medical service firms enter this market; how will this impact traditional health care providers; what if any liability issues are created here for current health care providers, among others?

Straw Man Modeling Process: Tips for Success

To be really effective and optimize the straw man planning process, there are some suggestions to improve your success using this management tool:

- *Ensure a "bottoms-up" planning process—minimize the role of the organization's senior executive*

While the senior executive may set the initial tone and perhaps outline the objectives, he or she should not send a signal on their outcome preferences. It is fine to set boundaries and overall ground rules, but you do not want to stifle the idea creation process up front.

On the other hand, sometimes initial counsel is helpful. Years ago, I played a key role in managing a planning session for a leading telephone company. Our objective was to develop straw man business models for international business expansion. The team's planned efforts were to look at various country opportunities and identify straw man business directions and possible strategies. Results of the effort were to be presented to the board for approval. The CEO understood the process and provided only one message: focus only on overseas markets where human rights are not a major issue; otherwise the board will reject our proposal, notwithstanding its merits. That is the "tops-down" guidance you need and expect.

- *Don't stifle discussion and the creative process*

Participants should be encouraged to share ideas no matter how far out they may seem. You should emphasize there are no wrong answers here and participants are encouraged to "think out of the room." These sessions work particularly well when participants have diverse skills and backgrounds.

I have been involved in managing many of these sessions in the United States and overseas and in almost all cases found them to be productive when the creative process was not impeded.

Some years ago I assisted an international phone company that wanted to more directly meet the data, voice, and video needs of their major chemical sector clients. The questions at the time were what opportunities they should pursue, what new services they could offer, how they should be structured, and so on. While a formal report was developed, which was well received, many of the ideas developed—for example looking at hazmat support services, new regulatory compliance services, and so on—were developed in straw man modeling sessions with a mix of talented staff drawn from many levels of the organization.

- *Ensure all ideas are captured*

Frequently after these sessions, there may be discussions suggesting possible final straw man models, but the real opportunity, perhaps in the view of the CEO or other senior staff, may be an option that was not recommended during the session. Tracking and defending why certain straw man options are *not* recommended is always a good idea.

Keep in mind often many of the identified new straw man directions may not have been conceivable five or ten years ago. In the health care sector, for example, progress here is driven by megaspeed supercomputing, groundbreaking genetic research, and the urgent need to develop new disease solutions.

Clearly global entrepreneurial age forces are impacting and changing all sectors and all players, both large and small. The question is how. What changes are expected; how will today's players change; who will win here and who will lose; what new opportunities will emerge; how does this all evolve? These are representative critical issues, and there are many more. So what is the model here for this new business—who works with whom; what is the flow of products, information, and processes; how do existing players fit in here?

Whether we talk about the new personalized medicine sector, the movie rental business, retail shopping, or social networking, our warp-speed, entrepreneurial age drivers are demanding the need for new thinking and "modeling."

Conceptualizing new markets and business structures is tough; straw man models are valuable tools to understand and communicate both the basics and other insights, such as what are the financial flows, how does the business make money, and other data. My experience confirms most business professionals have minimal experience in understanding this essential entrepreneurial age tool. No "straw man modeling" college course exists, but in today's morphing of markets, this is an essential skill. I have addressed aspects of the straw man modeling process in classes I have taught, and my experience is this is well received and it can be learned.

⚜

Chapter 15

Management 101: Statistics, Analytics, and Keeping Score

Get your facts first, and then you can distort them as much as you please. Facts are stubborn, but statistics are more pliable.
Mark Twain

The Power of Statistics

I believe Winston Churchill hit the nail on the head, statistically speaking, when he said that *"...politicians and forecasters should have about the same skills ...the ability to foretell what will happen tomorrow, next month, next year, and to explain tomorrow why it did not happen."* I am convinced that no aspect of the management decision-making process is mangled or mishandled more than the area of statistics.

The British also have a popular saying that related to how government has used (or misused) the statistical process in describing the unemployment situation *"...there are lies, damned lies and government statistics."* In the government sector, misuse of statistics is rampant, as most of us know. If you doubt that, turn to C-SPAN sometime and watch our legislators create eloquent arguments defending contradictory positions using the exactly the same base of statistics.

I am always amazed at how statistics can be used to defend a proposal, a point of view, and motivate people to take action. The fact is statistics often have a life of their own and, in the hands of smart individuals, can be used to great advantage.

Most of us understand that if after flipping a coin ninety-nine times with only "heads" showing, that the probability of showing a "tail" on the next flip is 50 percent (it is always 50 percent unless you are using a strange coin).

And how about the doctor who was treating a seriously ill patient? Questioned on his chances for recovery, the doctor says 100 percent. The patient, now quite happy, replied he thought his disease was usually fatal. The doctor reassured him saying, "...statistics do show that nine out of ten patients die from the disease you have. Yours is the tenth case I've treated and my nine other patients have died so you're sure to get well."

The problem with the above is using statistics that confuse correlation with causality.

Suppose you want to develop a new computer model to predict when stock prices will rise. You select one hundred stocks, look at closing prices each week for the past ten years, and identify, during this period, what week each stock reached a new high price. Suppose you now look at the average hemline of women's dresses during this same period, and you see an expected rise and fall each season. Using a correlation analysis, all these data points would be entered into a model. If the rise and fall of stocks and hemlines closely track each other, we say they show "high correlation." If they do not track each other, we say they have "low correlation." Correlation is usually shown as a percent with an estimate showing the margin of error, e.g., correlation is 80 percent plus or minus 3 percent. What we are saying here is 77 to 83 percent of all stock and hemline directions track closely during the ten-year period. What we are *not* saying is there is a causality between these two events.

Now suppose you do the above analysis and it shows a correlation of 95 percent with a 2 percent error margin. Given the high correlation, it is seductive to conclude these two events are directly related, which they are not. And it is also seductive to use one to project the value of the other—rising hemlines do *not* mean stocks will rise.

It is seductive, as you can see by the above simple example, to assume that if events are correlated, there is a causal relationship that can be used to project future outcomes. The incorrect thinking here unfortunately is often used to support fallacious arguments.

Average Performance Is Not Acceptable

You are taught at an early age that not everyone is a superstar and is not expected to be one. Do your job, meet the job requirements, achieve average performance, and you should be fine and have a long productive career.

The reality of the situation is sometimes your feet may be in the oven, and your head may be in the refrigerator. Your average temperature is just fine, from a statistical perspective, but your body parts are obviously in serious trouble. The message in today's dynamic environment is clear. You need to understand, with precision, *all* facets of the management processes you are involved with to really measure performance, if you want to ensure all your body parts, so to speak, are to remain in workable condition.

For example, suppose you manage a sales group of twenty sales staff. Your weekly sales tracking shows each sales rep is meeting your targeted *average* sales goals. Business is on target. Suppose each sales rep sells three products, A, B, and C. Drilling down to the next level, you see overall sales of each of these products are also meeting your *average* sales targets, maybe exceeding these with certain sales reps. Overall *average* performance, you are doing fine.

But in today's dynamic, fiercely competitive markets, that is not good enough. What is the mix of products A, B, and C for each sales rep: how are customers migrating between products A, B and C; how are we meeting sales goals, i.e., are we selling more product B and C to displace our product A customers; to what extent is internal customer migration to higher-cost products, rather than capturing new customers driving sales? These are representative questions you need to ask, and there are more.

The question related to displacement of existing product A users by increased product B and C sales is a particularly important point, since this suggests the possibility of a product D, which is not offered by your company, but may be by a competitor.

Related to the above, keep three points in mind. First, remember the starting point here—sales targets were met, average performance was achieved, and senior management should be pleased. Maybe, but that is not good enough—remember my head in the oven analogy. The above thinking is what companies must adopt to meet today's entrepreneurial age challenges.

Second, this is obviously a simple example for discussion purposes. In reality, sales groups may have hundreds of sales staff selling many related product lines. Understanding the relationships between each of these products, customer buying preferences, customer needs, and so on is a complex process, often using predictive analytics and other statistical tools. And in smart, leading companies, you can be sure average performance, even if goals are being met, is not good enough.

Finally, we now have the ability to drill down to define and meet individual customer needs, and the concept of an *average* customer or *average* product is yesterday's thinking in many sectors. What that suggests is how we measure and track sales and performance will also change. Today we see the "80/20 rule" driving management—focus on ensuring we meet targets for the major products and largest customers, the 80 percent, and we will do fine meeting average sales targets. The result is the creation of new enterprises that are positioned to produce and manage products serving the "20"—one example is Amazon. Developing the management systems and analytics to track millions of small product sales is Amazon's competitive edge vis-à-vis Barnes and Noble. As the market develops for personalized medicine and other exciting emerging services, the ability to profitably address specific, individual niche market needs will be the new critical success factor—the *average* customer concept will be history. And I expect emerging companies to play a key role here following the lead of Amazon and others.

Next Generation Business Intelligence and Predictive Analysis Models: Where We Are Heading

Look at the aircraft industry. If a Boeing "supplier's supplier" has a problem, superb supply chain management ensures Boeing receives notification quickly, before it impacts the assembly line. These controls mitigate risk and optimize performance, and are the norm in leading companies. Going well beyond traditional data mining, we can now build "predictive" models, predicting future supplier and business performance.

Predictive analytics "engines" analyze historical performance and risk data, often real time, define future risk and performance drivers, and help management optimize performance and mitigate risk. These new predictive analytics tools go beyond traditional data mining, analyzing industry reports, government filings, trade press, and other sources to assess supplier "health," pending regulations, other "unstructured" data sources. These results can be seamlessly integrated with other management data to more accurately gauge supplier and production line risk and improve performance.

Companies in all sectors—insurance, health care, financial services, manufacturing, others—are adopting these new tools enabling "drill down" and improved management control. Capabilities of these new tools are impressive. For example, these tools help identify risk in underlying assets within complex collateralized debt obligations (CDOs); identify underlying and often unknown factors impacting the health care quality in medical institutions; help insurance firms and credit-rating agencies rate credit worthiness and investment risk; provide regulatory agencies with powerful new control and monitoring tools examining financial reporting, audit, and disparate external data sources. Industry leaders in many sectors are embracing these new risk mitigation and performance improvement statistical management tools.

The new predictive analytic-based business management tools now emerging in all sectors are "raising the bar" in how leading firms optimize business performance given today's rapidly changing, dynamic global markets. And these new tools are evolving quickly—adapting today's leading companies to embrace these new capabilities is today's Management 101 challenge.

I only briefly addressed new "Management 101" directions here and plan to address this further in an upcoming book. Given the ability of new analytic tools to dramatically improve productivity and help drive the creation of new business, I view this as an exciting area that will receive considerable attention in coming months.

Chapter 16

Entrepreneurial Leverage and "Shovel Ready" Projects; Perspectives for Policymakers

The one who adapts his policy to the times prospers, and likewise that the one whose policy clashes with the demands of the times does not.
Niccolo Machiavelli

The "Traditional" Business Called Government Policy

Throughout *Chopstick*, I have emphasized two key points. Traditional companies are under pressure and must change, develop new entrepreneurial perspectives and tools to survive, and grow in today's dynamic, changing global marketplace. And entrepreneurial firms must also change and adopt more traditional business management perspectives and tools to build sustainable, structured, agile organizations. Pretty simple concepts to understand; much more difficult to execute as I have hopefully shown.

But we focused on the business sector. Suppose you look at another traditional sector—government policy. Saying this another way, what if we view government policy through an entrepreneurial prism, maybe push the envelope a bit, and see what new perspectives emerge? Given the scale of our current economic problems, I see exciting opportunities in the policy arena to "think out of the room," developing new entrepreneurial solutions, driving job creation and economic growth. Certainly important enough to devote a chapter in *Chopstick* to explore some ideas. A good starting point is the concept of a "shovel ready project."

So What Exactly Is a "Shovel Ready" Project?

One key question is how and where to inject new investment into the economy to ensure real substantive and sustainable economic growth. We developed the concept of "shovel ready projects" to create jobs and help fuel economic growth. So what exactly are shovel ready projects?

The Committee on Transportation and Infrastructure's Rebuild America proposal in late 2008 allocated about $85 billion for shovel-ready projects to enhance transportation, environmental, water resources, and public buildings infrastructure. This allocation I and many others suspect may have included a few "bridge to nowhere" projects. The objective here is to create jobs, which is our critical need. But suppose you think more entrepreneurially here, look beyond creating "shovel" jobs, and focus on new sectors offering the highest economic growth opportunities—what would be the result?

A good starting point here is to look at how other countries fuel economic growth and improve global competitive position. What are shovel ready projects in these markets—bridges, roads, buildings, ports, or others? I think many will be surprised to see the differences here and how far behind we really are compared to other developing nations.

Driving Economic Growth with Information Policy Rather than Shoveling Dirt

Obviously I am exaggerating here to emphasize a point. Shovel ready projects play an important role, employ thousands of people at all levels and do get people working and make a strong contribution.

The fact is in many countries, government support for shovel ready projects means building next generation "knowledge highways," not just interstate highways, a key distinction. Jumpstart innovation to drive global market leadership. Forge creative, well-crafted national infrastructure policies to drive economic growth, which creates higher value-added jobs. That is the formula used by many leading countries. Look at what some other countries have accomplished with these policies.

Korea has been estimated to be least five years ahead of the United States offering next-generation, high-speed wireless applications, and I believe it is even further ahead given what I see emerging. A recent Cisco-sponsored study, looking at broadband penetration as a measure of "preparedness for the future," ranks the United States behind fourteen countries—we are tied with Latvia and Canada for fifteenth place. And the global leader in this study is South Korea. Broadband penetration helps support a robust technology-fueled, knowledge economy spurring innovation, spawning new industry sectors and companies.

Look at Malaysia's government-sponsored and supported MSC initiative started in 1996. Driven by the prime minister's office, the program has impressive results, attracting 2,006 companies representing about sixty-three thousand knowledge workers, or almost 90 percent of all workers within MSC-sponsored companies. To fully understand how well crafted "tops down" national policies can leverage innovation and entrepreneurial assets to create a knowledge economy, I suggest look over the Malaysia MSC program Web site,[47] particularly the "Malaysia Government 10 Point Guarantees" for all member companies. Look at some of the entrepreneurial support services provided here: MSC's five year "pioneer status" tax relief provision; the "MSC Grant Scheme" providing nonrepayable grants of up to 50 percent of total R&D program costs; and many other ancillary benefits. These provide a blueprint for how one leading knowledge economy defines what they consider shovel ready projects that should be funded to achieve economic growth and leadership in the global knowledge economy. Most important, this growth is funded by private investment supported by creative, entrepreneurially driven government policies. I believe that is a winning formula.

Another model I find most encouraging is Singapore's Intelligent Island initiative, first envisioned more than twenty years ago. Creating a wired nation with low cost, broadband access nationwide, the Singaporeans' national vision went well beyond just creating high-speed ubiquitous "pipes." Their objective, which they have achieved, is increasing, as they say "productivity and creativity, spurring policies and creative partnerships to promote economic growth." And what shovel ready projects did they target? One area was cargo transportation. In a feature article more than fifteen years ago, I described my experiences and observations working in the region at the time, noting that goods entering

Singapore needed about fifteen minutes to clear customs using their new highly efficient, fully integrated national information network—much faster than most U.S. ports at that time. In the same article, I also noted that the prime minister's IT2000 project proposed to reduce that time to five minutes by the year 2000.[48] I argued at the time that we needed to retool our "information superhighway" vision, move beyond "pipes," and create *knowledge* economy applications, if we were to maintain our global competitive edge. I would have preferred to have been wrong in what I projected, but I was not.

You may have seen recent announcements in the United States about "virtual wallet" services enabling you to use your mobile phone to pay restaurants or other retailers without the traditional "card swipe." They are coming. And for years, we have been discussing health care smart cards to store all your medical records, reducing health care costs and improving quality of care. They are also coming. But the national infrastructure supporting both of these "advanced" capabilities have been in place for years in Korea and other countries. And many more next-generation applications we talk about here have also been operational in these knowledge economies for some time.

Some believe we are doing just fine, making progress, entrepreneurial efforts are accelerating to spur innovation and economic growth. We *are* going in the right direction; the question is are we moving quickly enough. Today's economic challenges and the reach and scale of our global economy demand, in my view, more proactive "tops-down," creative national information policies that will reap economic benefits. We can and need to do more entrepreneurial thinking here, and I believe we have high upside potential here.

So what is the impact of *not* having an entrepreneurial-driven, knowledge economy that has parity with other leading nations? We are behind the curve, and this impacts our economic growth and ability to compete in the global economy. Take health care as an example. We spend about $4,178 per capita for health care in the United States, *more than two times* the median cost of $1,783 in OECD countries and much more than Switzerland, which is next on the list at $2,794. And U.S. hospitals, by all measures, are the most expensive in the world, spending about one-fourth of their total budget on administrative costs. In private U.S. hospitals, about one-third of all expenses look like what you may expect in a hotel business—costs for check-in, room service, reservations, meals, cleaning, and check out. Think about that the next time you "check in" to a hospital room.

Some argue that we offer higher quality health care services, so U.S. costs should be higher. But get past the rhetoric, and statistics tell a different story. Just look at one statistic that I find most troubling, infant mortality rates, where the United States ranked twenty-sixth in the world among all industrialized countries with 7.2 deaths per one thousand live births. Compare this to Japan, Norway, Finland, and Sweden, which are all under four, and the United Kingdom, Canada, and Germany at 5.9, 5.2 and 4.9, respectively. This is a sobering report card on our health care system, which is not yet on life support, but clearly needs resuscitation.

Small and Medium Companies: Play a Key Globalization Role

When we think about globalization, most believe only larger companies play a significant role. A closer look at the numbers tells a different story with emerging early-stage firms also moving globally.

Based on Department of Commerce statistics, in 2003, about 225,190 U.S. companies are exporting products and services, doubling since 1993. Of the total, *about 97 percent* or 218,382 companies were small and medium companies. And of the total, *very* small companies (less than twenty employees) represented 69 percent or about two-thirds of all U.S. firms in the global market. Most do not realize that about two-thirds of all U.S. exporters are firms with less than twenty employees. And somewhere in this group, we may learn about several graduate students in a garage developing the next business success, in this case driven by market globalization forces.

So What New Ideas Should We Pursue, and Who Should Pursue Them?

In March 2008, I published an Op-Ed in the *Washington Post* offering a perspective on current economic challenges and some ideas to help rejuvenate the Washington, DC, regional economy. Emphasizing how entrepreneurial, emerging firms contribute to economic growth and the need to provide more support for these firms were the focus in the piece.

Overall reaction was positive, but I did receive comments, as expected, that my suggestion the government play a more direct role in nurturing emerging firms, particularly in strategic, knowledge economy sectors, was the *wrong* way to go. The private sector can and should carry the ball here was the message to me. That I view is *traditional* thinking, which really bounds the possibilities. We *do* have serious economic challenges; other countries are accelerating new initiatives *with* government support and doing well. What we need is *entrepreneurially driven* government support that promotes and encourages, rather than impedes, private sector involvement and investment. Difficult balance to achieve, but I and others see possible directions we can pursue here. *Entrepreneurial* rather than *traditional* thinking, maybe a dose of "thinking out of the room" is the prescription to win here.

As for what I suggested, while I and others felt I was on target here, there were people who believe this is not how we should proceed. You can be the judge on whether what I suggested is reasonable or the wrong approach. Here is a full copy of the Op-Ed:[49]

Paul B. Silverman

Washington Post

Monday, March 3, 2008; Page D03

New Ideas Needed as Jobs Shift

Take a look at the state of metropolitan Washington's knowledge-based economy.

The good news: Government contracts these days account for about 50 percent of all local high-technology business, growing annually at about 6.7 percent. High-tech employment ranks higher than in most U.S. regions. The bad news: The region is losing some of its key leadership and important jobs. AOL corporate executives are moving to New York. The company is eliminating 750 jobs in Northern Virginia. Sprint is moving its Reston headquarters to Overland Park, Kan., and cutting its local workforce.

Our challenge is to broaden the region's economic base and create new jobs to replace the old ones. To do that, we need some new solutions. Maybe we can learn something from efforts underway in Canada, China and other nations.

Start with Ontario. The Canadian province has lost 174,000 manufacturing jobs since 2002. To create jobs, the province chose to target telecommunications and biotechnology. But that takes investment, and venture capital was not forthcoming, dropping to $1.6 billion in 2006, from $2.2 billion in 2005. The solution? The Ontario government in November 2007 launched a venture fund that will invest

$270 million in "fledgling, entrepreneurial" companies. Why the focus on entrepreneurial-stage companies? Small- to medium-size enterprises with fewer than 100 employees account for about 48 percent of Canada's total workforce and in 2003 accounted for 23 percent of the country's research and development expenditures. Canada has many programs supporting growth in this sector and is reorienting others. One in particular, the 60-year-old industrial research assistance program, recently refocused its goals to increase the innovative capabilities of small- and medium-size businesses, helping them to grow and launch new products.

Now look at China, whose economic success was not achieved by accident, but through national policies promoting targeted economic growth. For example, in a smaller but resource-rich region, Jilin province in northeast China, the government is pursuing a comprehensive plan to create 10,000 mostly small- and medium-size companies each year through 2009, hoping to create 100,000 new jobs. The rationale is that China's smaller businesses drive economic growth, employing about 75 percent of all urban employees, holding about 60 percent of all invention patents and accounting for about 80 percent of new products.

Whether it be South Africa or Japan, other nations are following the same plan.

So why not here? Providing targeted assistance to emerging companies would not only help diversify our regional economy but also add to the tax base. Imagine 50 emerging firms, each with sales of $5 million. Helping those firms increase their annual growth to 20 to 30 percent adds $361 million in revenue over five years, driving job growth, increasing tax revenues and, most important, creating a more diversified, knowledge-based regional economy.

Some say existing venture capital and government programs can drive this growth. But venture capital funds less than 3 percent of the deals reviewed, take six months or more to make funding decisions and don't invest based on metrics such as whether the region benefits or jobs are created. And current government programs do not go far enough.

We should not take our global leadership for granted. Remember, the United States was once considered the worldwide leader in education. A 2003 UNICEF study ranked us 18th in education. South Korea, Japan and Singapore are ranked first, second and third, respectively. To ensure we do not lose our competitive edge in the rapidly evolving global knowledge economy, we can and must do better.

Playing Catch-Up in the Global Economy: Time for Action Is Now

Our economic challenges are formidable; getting people back to work and jumpstarting our economy must be a national priority. Meeting this target demands cohesive, national, "entrepreneurial-driven" policies looking beyond shovel ready projects, ensuring leadership in the global knowledge economy. Crafting cohesive policies balancing public and private investment, creating new ways to efficiently move goods and services, creating new solutions addressing today's health care and education challenges—these should be our targets. Other leading global players have made good progress here, and learning from these experiences can help us create an entrepreneurial-driven knowledge economy.

Good words here, but how do we make this happen? How do we best move from "pipes," infrastructure, and shovel ready projects to create new applications, drive productivity improvements, and economic growth? How do we forge creative entrepreneurial programs to jumpstart new jobs and economic growth in our cities, one of our nation's toughest economic challenges?

Let me share one program I developed about four years ago and, with a colleague, proposed to a social services agency as a strategy to address inner city needs and help jumpstart economic rejuvenation of our cities.

Representative Entrepreneurial Empowerment Program (EEP)

The thinking here was to create a tightly focused, short-term entrepreneurial education and mentoring program to help inner city entrepreneurs, both young and old, start and grow new business ventures. The program was comprehensive, going well beyond the scope of traditional start your own business seminars offered within adult education programs and universities.

The new Entrepreneurial Empowerment Program was developed to achieve four objectives:

1. To provide the lower-income community with new resources to explore their interest in pursuing potential new business opportunities
2. To create a fully integrated new business development program to support the planning, evaluation, business launch, monitoring, control, and support for a new business venture
3. To fully integrate the private sector and corporate sponsors to provide staff coaching and mentoring resources, matching funding, support services, and potential alliances for selected new ventures
4. To provide clients with the opportunity to identify, develop, and pursue larger scale high-potential opportunities

Note the use of the term "client" was intentional. The objective here is entrepreneurial *empowerment,* not a handout, and "client" sends the right signal here.

To target lower-income community clients, the new program was proposed to be offered within the Community Outreach Program, enabling clients to use existing Individual Development Account (IDA) funding to pursue new ventures. The EEP also linked in potential funding support from corporate sponsors and other sources. Going well beyond traditional entrepreneurship seminars, the program included formal mechanisms to screen and track new ventures and, where needed, provided management support via the EEP Business Mentor Program. Most importantly, the structure was scalable. Start in a neighborhood, expand to other neighborhoods, counties, regions, and so on.

The formula here—fully integrated, "tops-down" program structure; neighborhood level "bottoms-up" support; strong private/public partnerships; scalable, clearly defined metrics for all to understand and communicate—these are the features we need to emphasize as we develop other entrepreneurial programs to fuel economic growth.

The program also included a formal process to track new venture performance, as well as provide staff resources through the EEP Business Mentor Program to assist each new business venture and address critical business issues as they develop.

Summarizing, the proposed EEP structure enabled lower-income clients to pursue their new venture development activities within a formal, structured process with defined program metrics, and an ongoing management and control process.

The above Entrepreneurial Empowerment Program is one example of the entrepreneurial programs I envision that can make a real difference, help address our inner-city economic problems, and contribute to economic growth.

I have since evolved the basic structure to serve as a possible blueprint to help jumpstart economic development in less developed countries. Providing a balanced mix of entrepreneurial education, new venture screening, well-defined management and control processes, mentoring and funding with a strong public/private partnership is a winning formula. Having been directly involved working with selected overseas administrations that "think entrepreneurially," I am confident we can successfully pursue similar initiatives in the United States.

What I shared are representative of the opportunities I foresee when I suggest creating new government policy looking through an "entrepreneurial prism."

Time is of the essence. We cannot wait years to jumpstart our economy. Some may recall the words of the famous TV detective Charlie Chan who was always in motion and under attack: " I feel like a man trying to set a clock while its running—better to keep moving to stay ahead." That pretty well sums up where we are today.

∝✠✿

Chapter 17

Today's Information Age Revolution: We Have Faced "Tsunami" Market Challenges Before

A revolution is a struggle between the past and the future.
Fidel Castro

The Revolution in 1939: Book Industry in Transition

Today's entrepreneurial age challenges may seem formidable, incomprehensible, and threatening, but we have faced challenges in the past, many more ominous, and we have endured. The message here is we will meet today's challenges, and new opportunities will emerge as a result, many of which are not even on today's radar screens.

Many people compare today's entrepreneurial age revolution to a giant tsunami, threatening to swamp all, sweeping out anything in its way, reshaping the existing landscape, so to speak, mercilessly. Overwhelming, incomprehensible, like "grabbing a tiger by the tail," is how many view their attempts to keep up with today's explosive entrepreneurial age-driven changes.

New services offering "any information, anywhere, any time" are really fueling the entrepreneurial age revolution. And industry pundits emphasize this *is* a real revolution, with profound, far-reaching, unpredictable, even sinister results as privacy is impacted and our "digital shadow" is publicized for all to observe. These explosive changes are proliferating, unlike anything we have ever seen before. But wait one minute. Before we jump to conclusions about the end of the world as we know it today, let's put this into historical perspective.

We have, in fact, done this before, faced other so-called revolutions reshaping how information flows, and we survived and even learned a lesson or two. The last revolution occurred about seven decades ago, in the year 1939, with the start of the information "mass market." I find the similarities between today's market dynamics and the information landscape in 1939 striking, and there are lessons to be learned here. Let's go back in time for a moment and take a look.

Imagine that books—the information "lifeblood" of a democratic state in the PIE (pre-Internet era)—could only be purchased in about five thousand stores across the country—mostly gift shops and stationery stores selling just a few popular titles. And only about five hundred of these are legitimate bookstores, not like today's megabookstores, but really boutiques, selling jewelry and cut flowers, and catering to upper-class customers in the nation's twelve largest cities. And these legitimate bookstores are the *only* retail stores actually visited by publishers' salesmen. The results? Minimal mass market penetration. No bookstores of any kind in two-thirds of all counties in the United States. Half the books produced selling less than 2,500 copies across the country.[50]

Today we may look at these statistics with some disbelief—surely the mass market for books has existed at the turn of the century, or even during the 1800s, driven by enlightened immigrants reaching our shores. Nope. Strange as it may seem, with war on the horizon, 1939 was indeed the starting point for the last great information revolution. And like today, there were skeptics that attacked every proposal, fought to maintain the status quo, and preserve the vested interests. And there were also many failures; changing the way information is packaged, distributed, priced, and sold to the public was then, as it is today, a daunting multifaceted challenge. But as today, there were also heroes, whose vision and drive fueled the last information revolution, ultimately changing us all.

The revolutionary premise at the time went something like this; there is a massive, untapped market for low-cost books offered through new, creative consumer-marketing distribution channels. And the assumption, unproven at that time, was that such a new market could actually be highly profitable. This sounds close to the arguments we hear today about a viable, potentially profitable, mass market for e-books.

Going back to 1939 and peeling the onion on the problems, I believe, provides powerful insights on today's entrepreneurial age challenges. Some publishers recognized the need for low-cost "mass market" books, but did not want to impact sales of existing "trade" sales. A typical question at that time; "How can you make a profit on a twenty-five-cent book and not impact existing book sales?" Some publishers believed the masses were not "readers," what was called the "elitist convention." Another issue was the information quality vs. information "reach" tradeoff—i.e., if we streamline information to reach the masses, how do we maintain our existing high-quality standards? This sounds like the same problems of today, with pressures on major publishers to offer no-cost Internet-based content, while earning profits from their high-cost intellectual capital. There were many missteps and failures addressing this emerging market.

As early as the nineteenth century, there were attempts to "mass market" softcover books. Referred to as "penny dreadfuls" or "dime novels," most were sensationalized fiction and missed the mark. In early 1930s, attempts to market lower-cost "mass market" books also failed at prices in the thirty-nine to forty-nine cent range.

But in 1939 something happened that was the tipping point.[51]

On June 19, 1939, the book publishing "bomb" hit. Ten new titles were launched by Robert de Graff, an experienced, visionary publisher.[52]

Calling the series "Pocket Books," de Graff's formula for success was radical at that time: sell the new books as if they were magazines, using drugstores, newsstands, and even bookstores. Sell in large quantities, keep production costs low, increase production runs by minimum factor of ten, and target the price at twenty-five cents, to even offer readers a competitive alternative to lending libraries charging five cents a day (yes, you used to pay for this service). Recognizing the problems of earlier failed "pay less, get less" market entries, de Graaf emphasized "complete and unabridged" to offset criticism. The results? A great success, averaging twelve thousand to fifteen thousand copies per day with cigar stands selling one hundred to five thousand copies in first day. And the timing of the war and the tremendous demand for "pocketable" books no doubt helped fuel demand.[53]

Many previous attempts failed, but Pocket Books obviously had the right formula or "market mix." The critical success factors—reduce royalties to authors and hardcover houses, reduce dealer discounts, reduce binding and printing costs. Pocket Books sales increased to $8.5 million by 1941, a breakthrough success story launching the last information revolution.

But it was a rocky road, with many potholes on the evolving information highway. Paperback books also had their share of critics, despite the obvious explosive sales growth. Covers too lurid and unsuitable for children, "profanity," "cheap pulp material," and so on were the comments of the day. Remember books enjoyed elitist positioning at that time, and in many cities, police actually patrolled the newsstands, ready to seize any books deemed obscene (sort of like today's "Internet police"). Booksellers complained paperbacks took up too much space and did not provide the profit of hardcover books. Librarians complained they did not know how to catalog them. And many of the entrenched publishers, feared impacting the existing, well-established industry structure, did not want to upset the existing retail distribution channels. You can see the parallels here with today's e-book revolution.

Surviving Tsunami Market Challenges

But the traditional book publishers did not go out of business as the paperback market matured. Coexistence and adaptation were the norm, as we see in most sectors. I use the paperback market evolution in both the classroom and in other ways to show what I believe are striking parallels with today's market challenges and developments.

As many of us involved in today's entrepreneurial age revolution know, our challenge is to develop new business models to "slice and dice" valuable, proprietary intellectual capital, maintain quality, and meet market penetration and reach objectives. No small task given the challenges, but we have done this before and survived.

⚘

Chapter 18

Some Final Thoughts

Great is the art of beginning, but greater is the art of ending.
Henry Wadsworth Longfellow

I hope you have enjoyed our journey through *Chopstick*, perhaps learned a new idea or two, maybe developed some new perspectives, challenged your traditional thinking. I would like to share some final thoughts I believe are important to further reinforce many of the concepts discussed in *Chopstick*.

Perspective: Four Blind Men and the Elephant—It Only Looks Like an Island from the Water

One thread that runs through *Chopstick* is perspective. How you look at and react to business situations, respond to changing business dynamics, view market attractiveness—perspective shapes how you process and respond to these.

There is an old Indian parable that relates the tale of four blind men approaching an elephant for the first time. Each man feels a different part of elephant and is asked to describe what he is touching. The first man says he feels a large round stump and says it feels like a tree. The next man feels what he believes is a sock filled with rocks and so on it goes. Each views the elephant from his own perspective, draws his own conclusions, reinforcing the point that our ability to think and address problems really depends on our perspective, where we stand today and the road we took to get there. As the parable goes, they are not even sure they are touching an elephant. This simple yet entertaining parable communicates significant messages.

Today's entrepreneurial age is adapting our perspective and how we think in many ways. Take, for example, telling time. One of my favorite writers, the late Isaac Asimov, provides some fascinating ideas about the impact of the digital watch revolution and how it changes our day-to-day world. How many times do we refer to movement as clockwise or counterclockwise, terms we have grown up with, that form the basis for our perspective, defining how we may stand in line, describe the flow of water, or some other event. And how many of us, including boaters such as myself, use the clock system saying "fish at eleven o'clock" or "buoy at four o'clock." In today's digital watch world, these terms mean nothing. Imagine today's children, ingrained with digital watches from birth, not having exposure to dial watches, trying to understand what are we talking about here.

Other changes are less subtle, such as valuing a new venture. Suppose today you are offered an opportunity to join or invest in a new social network. The business proposes to establish a shared website, attract members, enter personal data, maybe participate in weight loss programs and competitions, perhaps offer educational games, and so on. All services are offered for free, and the plan is to attract users and sell advertising and, in the future, use analytics to create and sell information services and products to third parties. Today, with our social-networking explosion, successes such as Facebook and others, we understand and accept the value creation model here even though services are offered for free. Back up the clock five years or so ago, and that would not be the case.

And this leads to the next exciting business model I see emerging, what I call the "data intensity" model, where the *depth* of user information enables companies to offer users services that add significant value, going well beyond social interaction. These models create significant value and represent, based on my experience, an exciting emerging market. Again, that view is driven by *today's* perspective and what we have learned.

Summarizing, perspective is a powerful, insidious concept. Perspective can help people win or lose. Look at a problem and think it is hopeless, and it probably will be. But look at it with a winning attitude, and odds are you may be successful in solving it. I am not proposing you adopt a Pollyanna attitude here. Nor am I suggesting that *"sincerity is the most important thing...if you can fake that you've got it made"* as said by the late George Burns. No, the challenge is calling it like it is and understanding with some level of precision the impact of your decisions. But like the four blind men and the elephant, perspective is always driven from where we stand. So what we think is correct, and is the ideal choice, really only depends on where we sit and "what part of the elephant" we are looking at and touching at any given time.

Where we stand, our perspective, may, for example, define whether what we are looking at is a threat or an opportunity. In other words, maybe we are on the wrong side of the elephant, holding the "sack of rocks" when we are really seeking the " the tree stump."

Learning: The Counsel of Taxi Drivers

Like many others, I consider myself fortunate to have worked with some outstanding people—at all levels—in many diverse global organizations. Interaction with these individuals was a learning experience—make no mistake about it. While I have met with senior management staff in virtually every corner of the globe, you may find it surprising that one of my more memorable discussions occurred years ago with a Chinese cab driver in Singapore, providing me with his insight into the social pressures in Singapore, the cultural divide between the Malay and Chinese citizens, the impact of foreigners, the changing value system, how owning a Mercedes changes social positioning, and what he foresees are the *real* needs of the Singaporeans. I learned more as we passed the historic Raffles Hotel and wheeled through the streets of Singapore than at the meeting I was en route to with one of the senior government ministers.

I have observed that we can learn a great deal from those around us, at all levels. The starting point is to establish your own frame of reference and a value system that works, enabling you to chart a course and navigate through the really tough challenges we all face. You will get much advice, but my message here is simple: don't forget the counsel of the taxi driver and others who often provide valuable and unexpected insights on the world around us.

Is Entrepreneurship a Strategy, Process, Destination, or a State of Mind?

Bear with me here a moment and this should be clear. At the 1999 World Economic Forum annual meeting in Davos, Switzerland, the topic of globalization dominated the discussions. As reported by *Newsweek* and others, a new term was introduced at that meeting: "globality." The reasoning, expressed by Daniel Yergin, co-author of *The Commanding Heights,* and others at the meeting, was globalization is really a process, and you need a different term to define the results of the process. And these results go well beyond just economic impact and affect all dimensions of a country or region. Meeting attendees reviewed other attributes of the term *globality.*

I see a similar situation today in the entrepreneurship arena. Within *Chopstick,* I have shared ideas on what I call "entrepreneurial thinking"; mentioned the term "entrepreneurial age" numerous times (too many based on editor comments); emphasized the need to "think entrepreneurially" to meet today's challenges and so on. Looking back at the World Economic Forum discussions, I see parallels here. Just as we have seen with globalization, we have entrepreneurship terminology issues. How do we measure the *benefits* entrepreneurial thinking achieved; how do we compare two companies or perhaps regions or even countries to gauge how well the respective entrepreneurial strategies, policies, and programs worked; what are the milestones or destinations we need to measure progress?

Looking back at the World Economic Forum session, the same questions were raised about globalization driving the emergence of the new term "globality," referring to the situation emerging as a *result* of globalization forces. Replace the terms "globalization" with "entrepreneurship," and I think you will see my point.

What I envision is a new term—*entrepreneurality*—providing a clear distinction between the entrepreneurial *process* and the *results* of the process. Just as we have seen in the World Forum discussions, the new term enables us to develop benchmark metrics that compare the *results* of alternative programs across regions and perhaps countries and to rank entities. We will see whether this term catches on. Sounds like it may be a good title for a future book.

Entrepreneurial Firms: Like Football or Basketball Teams?

One of the more interesting management observations shared with me by an old and insightful friend years ago suggested a comparison between football and basketball teams. In both professional sports, players train intensely to meet tough standards and "keep their position" so to speak. But football players must know where they are and what to do at every step in a play, implying the need for structure, plans, and a well-organized blueprint showing "what-ifs" as the defense responds. Basketball, on the other hand, is a different game where individuals, for the most part, use "moves" to gain a competitive edge and score. Sure there are plays, and the ball is worked together as a team, but these differences hold true for the most part.

So the question posed by my friend was the following: to what extent are today's winning entrepreneurial age firms more like a basketball or football team? Follow this logic, and you realize that *successful* entrepreneurial age firms are indeed more like a basketball team structure: more degrees of freedom for staff, more forgiving, and while teamwork is obviously essential, individuals can soar. More traditional, established companies mirror the football team profile, however, where each player knows the rules, knows the boundaries on what can be done, and *works the plays*. Obviously there are many exceptions and this looks like a generalization, but it is surprising how often this perspective applies in examining many organizations.

Finding a Place to Stand

Today we also talk about explosive technology changes creating an upheaval of just about every traditional approach to conducting business or day-to-day living. And by all measures, the impact of information and computer technology has *only just begun.* Andy Grove, Intel's founder, estimated that so far we have achieved less than 5 percent of the Internet's real business and personal impact, implying 95 percent of the real opportunity and changes lie ahead. I and many others strongly agree; working with new technologies and ventures in health care and other sectors, I see exciting, emerging markets on the horizon that we are only thinking about today.

It is often easy to "believe your own snake oil" and assume new technology is always successful. As do most of us that see what I call "receding hockey stick" new venture revenue forecasts, we all know there is a high-risk road to *overestimating* technology's success, a point driven home by the crash in value of many 401(K) accounts that bet on virtually any technology-driven investment in the past decade.

But keep in mind there is also high risk to *underestimating* the impact of technology, overreacting by tempering the technology opportunities with traditional experience and perceived business realities. I have done this on occasion myself and recall one meeting many years ago when working with a leading communications services firm. Discussing the outlook for the Internet, which at the time was a noncommercial, global research network, my team and I concluded the Internet would always be limited to noncommercial applications given security and network management issues, while *real* commercial applications will continue to be handled by traditional communications firms. We didn't quite get that right.

I also particularly like the following "educated," often quoted insights from recognized industry experts:

"I think there is a world market for maybe five computers."
Thomas Watson, IBM Chairman, 1943

"I have traveled the length and breadth of this country and talked with the best people, and I can assure you that data processing is a fad that won't last out the year."
Editor of Business Books for Prentice Hall, 1957

"But what is it (computer chip) good for?"
Engineer at the Advanced Computing
Systems Division of IBM, 1968

"There is no reason anyone would want a computer in their home."
Ken Olson, Founder, President, and Chairman
of Digital Equipment Corporation, 1977

Think for a moment at the respective leadership role of each of these business leaders and the significant position each of their companies held in the market. Traditional firms, while they may be market leaders, do get it wrong sometimes, as I emphasized throughout *Chopstick*. I also expect these folks have probably regretted their past strategic visions. So how do you win? How do we measure what works, what doesn't, and where we can find a "place to stand"? If we accept Andy Grove's assessment, and I certainly do, there is a sense of urgency here, and creating successful future business models, finding a place to stand, will be even more challenging.

Ethics: The Narrow Line We Walk

To anyone who has been involved in managing large-scale business operations and worked in the global business arena, business ethics is and should be a primary driver for every action, large and small. I believe today's rapid-fire, explosive entrepreneurial age exacerbates the ethics challenges. The fact that most college courses now address the topic of ethics further reinforces its importance and why I included this in *Chopstick*. Each of us brings to the table our own set of values, ultimately shaping what we stand for and how we react when faced with the temptations. Management's ability to pursue what I call a "Triple A" business strategy (i.e., do anything, anywhere, anytime) is impeded by many factors, such as commercial laws, civil rights laws, and nerve-tingling legislation such as the Foreign Corrupt Practices Act (or FCPA as it is commonly called), threatening international executives with time behind barbed wire for acts of bribery, direct or indirect, in conducting business worldwide.

Your reputation is driven by your ethics, integrity, and character. You are judged by what you do, but just as importantly by how you do it and your guiding principles. The words of Ralph Waldo Emerson *"Who you are speaks so loudly I can't hear what you are saying"* provide excellent guidance to positively impact all those around you both in your business and personal lives. That is the roadmap I have always followed, and it works well. Your reputation is driven by your actions. Ethics, integrity, and character set the boundaries for life's highways—you have to stay between the lines.

What I have also found over the years are simple principles work best, and you need to pursue life's narrow road, with its many challenges, and "keep it between the lines." Not derived from an ancient philosopher, corporate manual, or an in-depth dissertation of the latest management principles, but rather from a country singer named Rickie Van Shelton in a song "Keep It between the Lines," which he released in 1991.[54]

Pretty simple really, and I hope and expect many readers have a similar set of principles. Categorized or said differently perhaps, but more or less the same idea. And maybe the final words in this chapter should come from a great leader who reigned more than three hundred years ago. As Napoleon Bonaparte observed, "Get your principles right and the rest is a matter of detail." I don't believe any of us could have said it any better.

Where We Go from Here

We obviously have survived one entrepreneurial-driven information revolution, and I have full confidence that we will survive today's entrepreneurial age challenges. To provide further comfort that we will endure despite today's problems and challenges, consider the following observations about other issues most can relate to:

> *"From the day your baby is born, said a famous scholar, you must teach him to do without things. Children today love luxury too much. They have inexecrable manners, flaunt authority, have no respect for their elders. They no longer rise when their parents or teachers enter the room. What kind of awful creatures will they be when they grow up?"*

While I am sure most can relate to this and it does fit right in with today's entrepreneurial age-driven "conspicuous consumption", the scholar who wrote this was Socrates shortly before his death in 399 B.C., more than two thousand years ago. Pretty sobering thought about how some things don't change all that much when you really think about it. And somehow we do survive. We all should appreciate what we do have and make the best of it. That is called success.

⚜

An Open Invitation

Within *Chopstick,* I have presented a number of ideas—some you may agree with; some you may not. I do hope you have enjoyed the journey.

I would like to hear your views and extend an open invitation to all readers to share your comments. You can always reach me on my blog *The NextGen Entrepreneurship Forum* via my Web site www.PaulBSilverman.com. I encourage you to share your views and will do my best to respond to all as time permits.

Thanks for reading and I look forward to hearing from you.

Paul B. Silverman

June 2011

About the Author

The author is well equipped to address this topic with four decades experience serving as public and private company CEO; entrepreneur; founder and former Director of the Entrepreneurial Step-Up Program at George Mason University; Adjunct Professor in the Center for Entrepreneurial Excellence ("CFEE") in the School of Business at George Washington University; mentor to senior executives worldwide. He currently serves as CEO of Sante Corporation, an early stage, leading edge personal health care management company that is developing a new vision to improve today's health care system. The author has also held senior management positions with RCA, GTE, Xerox and IBM (SBS), and served in senior global management consulting positions with Coopers & Lybrand, Booz Allen and Hamilton, and James Martin Strategy, where he served as CEO for North America. The author has conducted hundreds of presentations worldwide and published numerous articles addressing strategy, policy and new business development issues. The author holds a BS in Physics from CCNY and an MS in Management from Polytechnic University of NY, and resides in the Northern Virginia area.

❦

Endnotes

1. West Wireless Health Institute Study, Wireless Solutions for Health Care Reform, 8 Apr 2009, http://www.westwirelesshealth. org/images/white_paper.pdf (accessed October 1, 2010).

Introduction

2. For additional information on entrepreneurial management perspectives, I recommend reading Eric G. Flamholtz and Yvonne Randle, *Growing Pains: Transitioning from an Entrepreneurship to a Professionally Managed Firm- Fourth Edition*, (New York: Jossey-Bass, 2007), which I use as a supplemental textbook and frequently recommend to managers of early-stage firms.

3. Jeffrey A. Timmons and Stephen Spinelli, *New Venture Creation: Entrepreneurship for the 21st Century, Seventh Edition* (New York: McGraw Hill/Irwin, 2007), 54.

4. Timmons and Spinelli, *New Venture Creation*, 53–54.

5. Richard P. Feynman, *The Pleasure of Finding Things Out* (Cambridge, MA: Perseus Publishing, 1999), 146.

Chapter 1

6. General Motors Annual Report, 2009.

7. Google Corporation Annual Report, 2009.

8. ONSTAR is a registered trademark of General Motors Corporation.

Chapter 2

9. The "Three Legged Stool" model is adapted from the Timmons Model and analysis described in Timmons and Spinelli, *New Venture Creation*, 88–91.

10. Scotchguard and Post-It Notes are registered trademarks of 3M Corporation.

Chapter 3

11. ScotchGuard is a registered trademark of 3M Corporation.

12. Richard Conniff, "What the Luddites Really Fought Against," *Smithsonian Magazine*, March 2011.

13. Word and Excel are registered trademarks of Microsoft Corporation.

14 Richard N. Foster, *Innovation: The Attackers Advantage* (New York: Summitt Books, 1986), 139.

15. Foster, *Innovation*, 139.

16. To understand the challenges of disruptive technology and how an industry leader responds, I recommend reading "Kodak and the Digital Revolution (A)," Harvard Business School, Case No. 9-705-448, Revised November 2, 2005.

17. For those interested in understanding how TiVo impacted the DVD rental market, I recommend reviewing an excellent Harvard Business School case I frequently use: "TiVo 2007: DVRs and Beyond," Harvard Business School, Case No. 708-401, Revised December 20, 2007.

18. "W. L. Gore & Associates History Timeline," http://www.gore.com/timeline/.

19. Gore-Tex is a registered trademark of W. L. Gore & Associates.

20. Chris Anderson, *The Long Tail: Why The Future of Business Is Selling Less of More* (New York: Hyperion, 2006), 160.

21. Paul Gillin, *The New Influencers: A Marketer's Guide to the New Social Media* (Sanger, CA: Quill Driver Books, 2007), 115.

22. Gillin, *The New Influencers,* 130.

23. Gillin, *The New Influencers,* 129.

24. Gillin, *The New Influencers,* 70.

25. Ben Horowitz, "Notes on Leadership: Be Like Steve Jobs, ... And Bill Campbell, And Andy Grove," *TechCrunch*, March 14, 2010, http://techcrunch.com/2010/03/14/notes-on-leadership-jobs-grove-campbel/ (accessed September 15, 2010).

26. Ben Horowitz, "Notes on Leadership: Be Like Steve Jobs, ... And Bill Campbell, And Andy Grove," *TechCrunch*, March 14, 2010, http://techcrunch.com/2010/03/14/notes-on-leadership-jobs-grove-campbel/ (accessed September 15, 2010).

27. Several case studies provide excellent background in understanding the new venture development process, challenges, opportunities, and strategies. I recommend the following, which I have often used, reviewing a joint venture between Intel and SAP: "Pandesic—The Challenge of a New Business Venture (A)," Harvard Business School, Case No. 9-399-129, Revised August 30, 2005.

28. For an excellent discussion on corporate strategy, refer to Arie de Geus, *The Living Company: Habits for Survival in a Turbulent Business Environment* (Boston: Harvard Business School Press, 1997).

29. For an excellent review of how early-stage firms need to evolve to achieve growth objectives, I recommend reading Eric G. Flamholtz and Yvonne Randle, *Growing Pains: Transitioning from an Entrepreneurship to a Professionally Managed Firm, Fourth Edition* (New York: Jossey-Bass, 2007).

30. Many excellent strategy management books review Porter's Five Forces Analysis Model including Jay B. Barney and William S. Hesterly, *Strategic Management and Competitive Advantage-Concepts* (Upper Saddle River: Pearson/Prentice Hall, 2008). For further insight, I also recommend reading Michael Porter's initial paper describing the Five Forces Analysis Model: Michael E. Porter, "How Competitive Forces Shape Strategy," *Harvard Business Review: Strategic Management*, ed. Richard G. Hamermesh (New York: John Wiley & Sons, Inc., 1983), 35–49.

31. The cola wars provide excellent insights on strategy development by market leaders in highly competitive markets. I have used these often to examine the impact of alternative business strategies. For further information, I recommend reading a Harvard Business School Case Study: David B. Yoffie, "Cola Wars Continue: Coke and Pepsi in the Twenty-First Century," Harvard Business School, Case No. 9-702-442, July 30, 2002.

32. Charles W. L. Hill and Gareth R. Jones, *Strategic Management Theory: An Integrated Approach, Fifth Edition* (Boston: Houghton Mifflin Company, 2001), 139.

Chapter 12

33. Gary Dessler, *Management: Leading People and Organizations in the 21st Century: Second Edition* (Upper Saddle River, NJ: Prentice Hall, 2001), 30.

34. Dessler, *Management,* 31–32.

35. Dessler, *Management,* 32–33.

36. Dessler, *Management,* 33.

37. Dessler, *Management,* 35.

38. Dessler, *Management,* 35.

39. Dessler, *Management,* 36.

40. OXFAM, *Pass the Port: The Best After-Dinner Stories of the Famous* (Oxford, England: Christian Brann, Limited, 1976) 43.

Chapter 13

41. Hill and Jones, *Strategic Management Theory,* 270–271.

Chapter 15

42. Reprinted courtesy of Mobility Services International, 260 Merrimac Street, Newburyport, MA 01950-2192, USA, Mobility Services International, info@msimobility.com (e-mail). MSI offers excellent resources to assist in addressing global business issues, particularly related to human resource needs.

43. I recommend reading "General Electric Medical Systems (GEMS)," Harvard Business School, Case No. 703-902, which I often enhance based on my business experiences to review the challenges leading global corporations face when entering overseas markets. The HBS case is comprehensive and describes GE's experiences entering the China medical device market.

44. There are many excellent books on developing strategy-driven international corporate management structures. One I recommend is Arthur A. Thompson, Jr., A. J. Strickland III, *Strategic Management Concepts and Cases, Thirteenth Edition* (New York: McGraw Hill Irwin, 2003).

45. Charles W. L. Hill and Gareth R. Jones, *Strategic Management Theory, An Integrated Approach, Fifth Edition* (New York: Houghton Mifflin, 2001) 269.

46. "American Brands In Foreign Hands," http://247wallst.com/2010/10/08/american-brands-in-foreign-hands/, October 8, 2010

Chapter 16

47. The Malaysia MSC Program is an excellent example of how government policy structure and entrepreneurial incentives can be used to promote a knowledge economy driving innovation and job creation. For further information on the Malaysia MSC Program refer to http://www.mscmalaysia.my/topic/MSC+Malaysia+Bill+of+Guarantees.

48. Paul B. Silverman, "In Perspective: Information Management— The Great Schism, Parts 1 and 2," *Communications Week*, September 12, 1994.

49. Paul B. Silverman, "New Ideas Needed as Jobs Shift," *Washington Post*, March 3, 2008, D 03.

Chapter 17

50. Kenneth C. Davis, *Two-Bit Culture: The Paperbacking of America* (Houghton Mifflin Company: Boston, 1984), 16–17.

51. Ray Walters, *Paperback Talk* (Chicago: Academy Chicago Publishers, 1985), 2–3.

52. Walters, *Paperback Talk*, 4.

53. Walters, *Paperback Talk*, 5.

Chapter 18

54. "Keep It between the Lines" is a country music song written by Russell Smith and Cathy Louvin and recorded by American country music singer Ricky Van Shelton.

www.ingramcontent.com/pod-product-compliance
Lightning Source LLC
Chambersburg PA
CBHW032302210326
41520CB00047B/850